T0149653

MAKE LIFE COUNT

Maximizing Our Time on Earth

Larry A. Brookins

authorHOUSE®

AuthorHouse™
1663 Liberty Drive
Bloomington, IN 47403
www.authorhouse.com
Phone: 1 (800) 839-8640

Published by AuthorHouse 08/06/2018

ISBN: 978-1-5462-5471-3 (sc)
ISBN: 978-1-5462-5470-6 (e)

Library of Congress Control Number: 2018909277

Print information available on the last page.

DEDICATION

I dedicate this book to my sister, Charlotte M. Brookins-Hudson, who is also my editor. Charlotte is an amazing person who tirelessly gives herself in service to so many: her church, her family, her friends, her neighbors, and her God. Words cannot adequately express how grateful I am to you for your selfless collaboration on this book. You make me a better writer and the world a better place. Indeed Charlotte, you make your life count! Thank you for being who you are and for all you do.

CONTENTS

CONTENTS

ACKNOWLEDGMENTS

First of all, none of my accomplishments would be possible without the endowment of God's grace and inspiration. For this, I am forever humbled. For this, I am incessantly grateful. Secondly, as with previous book projects, I must acknowledge the incredible contributions of my editor and sister Charlotte M. Brookins-Hudson to whom this book is dedicated. Charlotte is my coach who perfects my writing flaws and enhances my message. "Thank you" Charlotte! I also want to thank my wife Sandra who gives me quiet time to write. Last, but not least, I want to thank my parents, my siblings, my children, and my church family and friends for any and all support provided to my ministry and business endeavors, especially my *L.A. Brookins Ministries* traveling crew: Renee K. Robinson, Patricia A. Johnson (sister), Charlotte M. Brookins-Hudson (sister), Clarence L. and Ann M. Brookins (brother & sister-in-law), and Sammie and Debra Robinson. God bless each of you! As always: BECAUSE OF CALVARY.

"You only live once, but if you do it right, once is enough."
Mae West

INTRODUCTION

Tick-tock, tick-tock. Tick-tock, tick-tock. This is the sound that a clock makes as it goes around its cycle of moving time. With each tick, we get older. With each tock, life is shifting us from one phase of life to another. With each new minute of each new day, what was is no more, and as time changes and the number of our years increase, the windows of possibilities dwindle. With this in mind, it is so important that we seize our days and take advantage of every prospect of time and life.

The Bible encourages us to 'redeem the time' (Ephesians 5:16), which means that we should "make the most of every opportunity" (NLT). With this in mind, it is imperative that we do not ignore or neglect any season of our lives, whether it be spring (adolescence), summer (young adulthood), fall (adulthood), or winter (old age). As the climate changes around us, so does the atmosphere within us. Before we know it, black hairs become gray, eyesight grows dim, the pace of our walk decelerates, and our skin wrinkles.

With every tick-tock of time, we get an audible reminder that moments are fleeting. With every ache in our bodies, we are prompted with the notice: "get it done," "do it now," "appropriate the season," "make life count." The thought of 'making life count' is the catalyst for this book. The thought of 'making life count' is the reason I am motivated to script the contemplations of my mind. Too many people waste time. Too many people spend too much time doing nothing concrete with their lives.

Why are we here? Are we here to simply occupy space? Why are we here? Are we here merely to gratify ourselves? Does life have meaning? Does life have purpose? Is there any point to human life? Is there any application for human life? Some would say, "we have no purpose but to exist." Some would say, "we are simply the byproducts of a cosmic collision." The latter are the "big bang" theorists. They claim that the universe began in an explosion and expanded over billions of years to what we know it to be now through biological evolution. However, this supposition dismisses God as Creator and, thus, God's purpose for our lives. We discuss the question of purpose and God in Chapter Two.

Let me simply say here, in making life count, we must have purpose. Can we have purpose without God? What meaning is there to life without God? From a Christian perspective, life has no meaning without God and we serve no purpose without God. An atheist may disagree, but an atheist denies or rejects the very idea that there is a God. From an atheistic view, why then are we here? From an atheistic view, what meaning is there to life? Rather than dismiss God, I dismiss the atheistic opinion. I say, emphatically, apart from God, there is no purpose or meaning to life. So then, why are we here? So then, what justifies our existence?

Like King Solomon, each of us should launch a full-scale existential investigation. In examining the Book of Ecclesiastes, in seeking purpose and meaning to life, Solomon begins with the prime observation: "All is vanity" (Ecclesiastes 1:2). In other words, "everything is meaningless" (NLT) apart from God. The word "vanity" in the context of Solomon's reflection means "useless." In Solomon's quest for answers he concludes: "Fear God and keep His commandments: for this is the whole duty of man" (Ecclesiastes 12:13). In his conclusion, Solomon, in his wisdom of research and experience, points everything to God and surmises that we should: enjoy life now and make the most of the opportunities that God gives us.

God is Creator. God is in control. Our lives are in His hands. God is the giver of life, the sustainer of life, the restorer of life, the meaning to life. Apart from God, life is monotonous, and wisdom is vain, and wealth is futile, and death is certain. The advice of Solomon: look up, look within, look ahead, and look around. The advice of Solomon: take into consideration time, eternity, death, and suffering. These are four factors that God uses to keep our lives from becoming monotonous and meaningless. In his final deduction and own implementation Solomon gives us four portraits to life and allocates to each portrait a practical admonition: 1) Life is an ADVENTURE, we should live life by faith, 2) Life is a GIFT, we should embrace it and enjoy it, 3) Life is a SCHOOL, we should learn from every lesson, and 4) Life is a STEWARDSHIP, we should reverence God, defer to His will, and use every resource to bring glory to His name.

How do we make life count? We start with God. How do we make life count? We stay with God. How do we make life count? We submit to God. How do we make life count? We end in God. This is the premise of this book. To maximize our time on earth we should: utilize time wisely, not put off what we can do, give ourselves in benefit to others, and leave an indelible mark along the paths of our footsteps. Whatever we do, we should strive to do the best that we can do. Whatever time we are allotted by God, we should make it quality time by investing it well in what God requires of us to do. What does God require of us? Micah 6:8 says, "To act justly and to love mercy and to walk humbly with your God" (NIV). As sure as you have life, breath, and body, make it count. Your life has purpose. Your story is important. Your years matter. You were born to make an impact. MAKE LIFE COUNT!

"Appreciate the gift of a new day, make it count as time
is of essence and every minute is a blessing."
Malika E. Nura

Chapter One

MAKING LIFE COUNT

Be careful how you live. Don't live like fools, but like those who are
wise. Make the most of every opportunity in these evil days.
Ephesians 5:15-16, NLT

The above statement is a passage from the Bible. Its writer
is the Apostle Paul, and its communication illuminates
the subject matter of lifestyle. In particular, it spotlights
the lifestyle of a Christian. What is lifestyle? Lifestyle
encompasses a person's habits, and attitudes, and
proclivities or inclinations, as well as a person's choices
and convictions. Overall, lifestyle has to do with the way
in which we live. In the Book of Ephesians, Chapter Four,
we are urged to "put off" a way of living that is associated
with the pre-Christian life in favor of living the type of life
in keeping with the paradigm of character and behavior
exemplified by Jesus. In Chapter Four of Ephesians, we
are advised to "put on the new man, which after God is
created in righteousness and true holiness" (v. 24).

True holiness is not a religion, but a lifestyle.
Righteousness has to do with being morally right. A
person becomes morally right by adhering to moral
principles, in particular, the moral principles outlined in
God's Word. In Chapter Four of Ephesians, Paul gives a

1

series of exhortations concerning a Christian's conduct. In Chapter Five of Ephesians, Paul continues these exhortations with a special emphasis on responsible living. What is responsible living? Responsible living is living one's life by a sense of duty, especially duty to God. It is living one's life in accordance with the highest standards of integrity and decency, godliness and goodness—living life carefully or thoughtfully, charitably and respectfully.

Amid a society that is becoming increasingly uncivil and immoral, unfriendly and wicked, there is a need for a people who will live responsible lives. Amid a society that is cold-blooded and careless and wasteful of life, we need people who will make life count. Making life count is taking full advantage of every opportunity we have to make a positive impact in this world. Making life count is doing something good with the time we are allotted in life to make life better for someone else. It is leaving a legacy of beneficial knowledge, deeds, values, and investments.

Time equates to life, and life is the period of time we inherit between birth and death. To put it another way, life is the overall timeframe of our existence. It is worth noting that in this current life, we only get one shot to make life count. We only get one shot to leave an imprint. We only get one shot to make an impact. We only get one shot to make a difference. We only get one shot to lay hold of time. If we waste time, we waste life. If we mismanage time, we mismanage life. Someone said, "Life is short. Time is fast. No replay. No rewind" (author unknown). Indeed, life is short, time is fast, and we get no replay and no rewind. Life is too short to squander, exploit, take for granted, or to treat with contempt. It is too precious. It is too irreplaceable. It is too limited. Life is too unpredictable.

None of us know how long we shall live. None of us know the actual date of our demise. One thing is certain, we all die. One thing is certain, none of us will stay here. We all have a destiny with the grave. We all have an appointment with death. None of us have the same longevity of life. None of us have the same length of years, months, weeks, days, minutes, and seconds. None of us come here and leave here together. But although our existences vary, one thing we have in common—we can all make life count. Making life count does not factor in how long we live, it factors in what we do with the years we live. Some people do not live long, but still they accomplish much. Some people live long, but they do little or nothing with their lives. It is not how long we live, but rather how well we live. It is not the amount of years we are given, but the effect we make with the years.

Muhammad Ali once said, "Don't count the days, make the days count." This means we should do something significant with our time. Remember: time equates to life, and we should make every moment of life as momentous as possible. Every day the beats of the pendulum of life becomes less and less and the window of opportunity gets smaller and more difficult. With this in mind, we ought not to waste much time wishing and hoping, but we should work toward doing something meaningful and fulfilling. We should maximize our time here on earth taking advantage of every moment of every day because every day life is ticking away one moment at a time. With this in mind, if we plan on doing something we should do it. We should not wait for something to happen. We should strive to make it happen. We should not just suck up air and take up space, but we should make a difference with our lives. We should make life count.

With our time on earth, we should help somebody. With our time on earth, we should serve somebody. With our time our earth, we should love somebody. With our time on earth, we should mentor somebody. We should teach somebody. We should reach out to somebody. We should inspire somebody. We should steer somebody to a saving relationship with Jesus Christ. We exist for a reason. Every life has purpose. No life is an accident. All life must count for something. Ephesians 5:15 says, "Don't live like fools" (NLT). Foolish people do not believe in God (Psalm 14:1). Foolish people do not live for God. Foolish people do not respect their neighbors. Foolish people mistreat their neighbors. A fool will steal. A fool will belittle. A fool will lie. A fool will kill. Fools do not value life, nor does a fool appreciate or grasp the true meaning of life. Fools abuse life only living to get drunk, or high, or to do things that are detrimental to life. Fools live life without prospect. No plans. No savings. No expectation. No organization. Fools live life recklessly without restraint. In order to make life count and maximize our time on earth, we cannot live like fools. Fools despise wisdom, repeat mistakes, do not think before they talk, and they do not care who they hurt. Do not be a fool!

Make life count. "Be careful how you live" (Ephesians 5:15 NLT). Be wise and not foolish. "Make the most of every opportunity" (Ephesians 5:16 NLT). We are living in evil days. Tomorrow is not promised to any of us. Each new day is a blessing. Each new day is a privilege. Each new day is grace given to us by God to get it right, to turn some things around, to let some things go, to embrace His will for our lives. To say to God: "Our Father, who art in Heaven, hallow be Thy name. Thy Kingdom come; Thy will be done" (Matthew 6:9-10). To say to God: "Lord, I surrender." I surrender my life. I surrender my will. I surrender my affection. I surrender my faithfulness. We ought not to disregard what God gives us with each new day. With each new day we have the opportunity to do better than we did and to become better than we were. We have the opportunity to repent of our sins of yesterday and to make amends with God and others. With each new day we have the opportunity to make life count.

With each new day we should do something we have not done before. We should work on something we want to achieve. Every life should have a bucket list and throughout life, we should endeavor to accomplish the things we catalogue to realize: go back to school, get a better job, start a business, etc. Whatever the dream and whatever the goal, we should utilize the time of today to enhance tomorrow. We should live while we have life. We should help somebody along the way. We should exhibit the light of Jesus Christ. We should lead somebody to salvation. We should honor God. We should do His will. We should share His Word. We should walk in His way. We should make life count. We should make an impact and we should make a difference. We should not simply exist, but we should maximize our moments.

Make life count. Do not just wake up. Make life count. The clock is ticking and time is winding up. James 4:14 reminds us: "Life is but a vapor." We are only here for a little while. Our lives are like a mist, or a puff, or like vanishing smoke, or fog in the morning. It is only brief or transitory. What we have is what we have. We have no guarantee of what comes next. We should not procrastinate, or delay, or defer, or take a raincheck. We should make life count. We should put God first (Matthew 6:33). We should make life count. We should love God with our whole heart, mind, soul, and strength (Luke 10:27). Without God, life has no purpose. Without God, our lives have no future. Make life count. Maximize your time here on earth. Make life count. Live life in God's purpose.

"Without God, life has no purpose, and without purpose, life has no meaning. Without meaning, life has no significance or hope."
Rick Warren

Chapter Two

LIVING IN GOD'S PURPOSE

Many are the plans in a man's heart, but it is
the LORD's purpose that prevails.
Proverbs 19:21 NIV

Every life has purpose. Every life is given life for a reason. No life is birthed into this world to simply exist. No life is brought forth into the realm of Planet Earth for nothing. All life has created purpose. Whether you agree or not and whether you understand or not, all life is meant to serve a purpose. No life is an accident. No life is coincidental. No life is unplanned. All life is intentional. A baby conceived may sometimes shock us, but never God. The news of "I'm pregnant" may traumatize some of us, but never God. No insemination or human life gestation surprises God. No matter how we got here, all life is born on purpose and for purpose. No matter what was done to generate an embryo within the womb of a woman, all human life is purposeful.

If there is no purpose for life, there is no meaning to life. If there is no purpose for life, our lives have no value. However, every life has value because each life is important. Every life has value because each life is significant. Even if you think you are not valuable, you are. Even if you feel that you do not have much to offer, you do. Whoever you are—you have worth. Whoever you are—you have purpose. You may not know your purpose, but still you have purpose. You may not occupy your purpose at present, but still you have purpose. None of us are here without purpose. There is function or assignment for every life—we must simply discover what it is. How do we discover our purpose?

In order to discover our function or assignment, we must begin with God. In detecting our purpose or reason of existence, we must look to God. We must read His Word and unearth His Will. We must come into relationship and fellowship with God. In relationship, there is disclosure. In fellowship, there is revelation. We begin with God and we look to God because all life is created by God. All life is created in God's image and in His likeness. All life is created with God's breath and for His purpose. For every life God has a specific plan. Jeremiah 29:11 says: "'For I know the plans I have for you,' declares the LORD, 'plans to prosper you and not to harm you, plans to give you hope and a future'" (NIV). For every life, the search for purpose culminates with God.

Without God, there can be no life. Without God, our existence is meaningless. Without God, our years are spent in vain. Without God, our lives lead only to the grave. That is it! Without God, the verdict upon every life is: "ashes to ashes, dust to dust, and earth to earth." If we live only to die the question becomes: "Why are we here?" Good question! Why are we here? If we cease to exist when we die, then what ultimate meaning can be given to life? If we cease to exist when we die, does it really matter that we existed? What is the significance of life without God? What is the goal of life without God? Our purpose in life is linked to God. Our purpose in life is apportioned by God. Therefore, we begin with God. Therefore, we look to God.

If we are to discern and fulfill our purpose in life, we must investigate God's will for our lives. All life exists because of God and all life finds its purpose in God. Therefore, we must live life in God's purpose. Living life in God's purpose is living life with purpose. It is doing something positive with one's life. It is doing something concrete or tangible with one's life. Living in God's purpose is making a difference in life. Living in God's purpose is making an impact upon lives. It is doing more than drinking, and partying, and getting high. It is doing more than watching television and playing video games. It is more than hoping and wishing. It is more than eating, sleeping, and living for the weekend. Living in God's purpose is when we truly make life count.

Living in God's purpose is lending a helping hand. Living in God's purpose is making life better for somebody else. Living in God's purpose is leaving a beneficial legacy behind. Living in God's purpose emerges when we utilize our gifts and talents and resources to inspire others. When we avoid reckless living, we live in God's purpose, and when our lives can bring glory to God, we live in God's purpose. In essence, as we go through life fulfilling the commands of Christ to feed the hungry, and shelter the homeless, and visit the sick and incarcerated, and provide ministry to the less fortunate among us, we live in God's purpose (Matthew 25). We are given life to enhance life. We are given life to convert life. We are given life to influence life. We are given life to accomplish

God's purpose for our lives. What is God's purpose for our lives? Good question!

God's purpose is people helping people. God's purpose is people loving people. God's purpose is people respecting people. God's purpose is people easing the burdens of other people. It is people being kind to one another. It is people being fair with each other. It is people being thoughtful and generous of one another. It is people with a willing heart to forgive. Ephesians 2:10 declares: "We are God's handiwork, created in Christ Jesus to do good works" (NIV). Interpretation: God fashions us to please Him, and to obey Him, and to acknowledge Him, and to live life on His terms. What are the terms of God? Another good question! In answering this, we go to the Ten Commandments in Exodus Chapter 20.

Term One: Put nothing or no one before God (Exodus 20:3). Term Two: Worship nothing or no one but God (Exodus 20:4-5). Term Three: Do not take the LORD's name in vain (Exodus 20:7). Term Four: Remember the Sabbath day, to keep it holy (Exodus 20:8). Term Five: Honor both father and mother (Exodus 20:12). Term Six: Do not murder (Exodus 20:13). Term Seven: Do not commit adultery (Exodus 20:14). Term Eight: Do not steal (Exodus 20:15). Term Nine: Do not bear false witness (Exodus 20:16). Term Ten: Do not covet what somebody else possesses (Exodus 20:17). Let us go through the list again. Put another way: term One: Put God first, term Two: Reverence only God, term Three: Keep God's name holy, term Four: Keep God's day holy, term Five: Respect your parents, term Six: Do not take another's life, term Seven: Do not have sex with someone else's husband or wife, term Eight: Do not shoplift, embezzle, pickpocket or cheat, term

Nine: Do not lie, and term Ten: Do not crave for yourself what other people have. In other words, leave their stuff alone. Living in God's purpose is living life on God's terms.

God's purpose for our lives is summed up in this: we should love God completely and love others as we do ourselves (Matthew 22:37-39). In this, we keep God's commandments (Matthew 22:40). In this, we fulfill God's purpose. In fulfilling God's purpose, our lives are made richer. In fulfilling God's purpose, we bring honor to God's name. In fulfilling God's purpose, we give meaning to our existence. In fulfilling God's purpose, our living is not in vain. When we help somebody as we pass along, and cheer somebody with a word or song, and show somebody that they are traveling wrong, our living is not in vain. When we do our duty as a Christian ought, and bring back beauty to a world up wrought, and share love's message as Jesus taught, our living is not in vain. Our living is not in vain if we care, give, serve, and lead somebody to a saving relationship with Jesus Christ.

Living in God's purpose is all about doing God's will. It is about living holy. It is about walking upright. It is about having a sense of duty. It is about our lives delighting God. If we delight God, we please God, and when we please God, God promises to give us the desires of our heart (Psalm 37:4). Living in God's purpose is rewarding, advantageous, advisable, and it justifies life. It justifies us being here. It justifies us staying here. It justifies us waking up. It justifies the totality of our existence. It justifies work. It justifies wealth. It justifies worship. It justifies God's Word: "Many are the plans in a person's heart, but it is the LORD's purpose that prevails" (Proverbs 19:21 NIV).

It is God's purpose that gives our lives purpose, and substance, and value, and makes life worth living. God's purpose augments life, and energizes life, and intensifies life, and it may, like in the case of King Hezekiah, extend life (2 Kings 20)—if not here, then beyond here. Living in God's purpose is the key to prolonged life, and to abundant life, and to favored life, and to everlasting life. It is the key to God's heart, and to God's ear, and to God's hand, and to God's blessings. When our lives please God, no weapon formed against us shall prosper (Isaiah 54:17). When our lives please God, no good thing will God withhold from us (Psalm 84:11). If we please God, God applauds us, and approves us, and commends us, and we shall hear Him say one day, "Well done."

If we are to make our lives count and maximize our time here on earth, we need to live life in God's purpose. We need to make an impact with our life and leave a legacy worth leaving. This would justify our existence. Our purpose is our destiny, calling, mission, and the reason we are here. It is why we are breathing. It is what we are gifted for. It is why we have flesh and bones. It is God's assignment for our lives. Do you know God's assignment for your life? Are you doing it? Will you do it? Will you complete it? Will you live your life in God's purpose? The meaning of life is finding our purpose. The purpose of life is a life of purpose. Remember: all life is created on purpose. Remember: all life is created with purpose. Remember: all life is created for purpose. Remember: all life should be lived in purpose. Live it! Do it! Fulfill it! Live life in God's purpose and live it with no limits!

"Limitations live only in our minds. But if we use our
imaginations, our possibilities become limitless."
Jamie Paolinetti

Chapter Three

LIVING WITH NO LIMITS

Jesus said to him, "If you can believe, all things
are possible to him who believes."
Mark 9:23 NKJV

Without delving into the background of Mark 9:23, I want
to focus on the words of Jesus: "If you can believe, all
things are possible to him who believes" (NKJV). This
statement by Jesus affirms the potential and power of
faith. Faith, by definition, is "a strong belief in something
for which there is no quantifiable corroboration or proof."
Faith is conviction without evidence. Faith is confidence
without authentication.

Faith is essential within our lives as Christians. It is
faith that brings God onto the scene of our situations and
aspirations. God shows up where faith is present because
faith is a demonstration of our acceptance of God and
acknowledgment of what God is able to do. Where faith is
present, there are no restrictions on God's ability. Where
faith is present, what can be manifested or accomplished
has no limitation.

Faith in God rejects the idea of limit. Faith in God
vetoes the very suggestion that there are boundaries
to what is possible. Faith in God supplants any form of

misgiving. Faith in God uproots all seeds of distrust and doubt. Faith disbelieves naysayers and faith disregards the communication of scoffers and skeptics. Faith, that is faith, absolutely believes God. This kind of faith is the kind that is crucial if we are ever to experience what is atypical in our realm of what is ordinary or commonplace.

When Jesus says, "All things are possible to him who believes," the assertion is: with faith, nothing is impossible. In saying, "nothing is impossible," we are saying that nothing is unattainable, unfeasible, impractical, or insurmountable. What can be conceived and believed, with God, it can be achieved. In the spirit realm of faith, there are no remote possibilities, or long shots, or improbabilities, or lotteries. We take no chance having faith in God. We roll no dice believing that nothing is too hard for God. What is it God cannot do? What is it God cannot bring to pass?

In Ephesians 3:20 it is written: "Now unto Him that is able to do exceeding abundantly above all that we ask or think, according to the power that worketh in us." What is this "power that worketh in us?" The power that worketh in us is our faith in God. Without faith, we nullify God's abilities. Without faith, we prevent God from intervening in our lives. God honors faith and He does so because faith honors Him. A lack of faith discredits God. A lack of faith disparages the omnipotence of God.

God is all-powerful. This is what "omnipotent" means. *Omnipotent* is defined as: "unlimited power; able to do anything." This definition describes God and can only be applied to God. Only God is able to do anything. We simply must believe it, accept it as true, and conduct ourselves accordingly. It does not matter what odds are against us. It does not matter what barriers lie before us. With faith, nothing is impossible. Faith esteems God. Faith concedes to God. Faith does not waver and it does not compromise. Faith does not seek an alternative plan—faith sticks with God. This is the kind of faith that enables us to live with no limits.

In living with the mindset of no limits we tell ourselves: "I can do it." We tell ourselves: "I will pursue it." We tell ourselves: "I will complete it." We tell ourselves: "It shall come to pass." With this belief we let no one discourage us, dissuade us, unsettle us, or put limits on us. We plan. We go for it. We endeavor to make things happen. We do not give up along the way. Our philosophy is: "If it does not work the first time, we try again," and "if one door is closed, we knock on another." We serve a God of no limits. There is nothing God cannot do or make a reality in our lives. Romans 8:31 declares: "If God be for us, who can be against us?"

All things are possible with faith. The problem arises when we allow circumstances to frustrate our faith. The problem arises when we abandon our faith during hard times. All faith will meet challenge, but true faith perseveres. True faith weathers the storm. True faith continues. True faith endures. True faith yet believes in spite of. In spite of conditions. In spite of surroundings. In spite of obstacles. In spite of adversities. True faith keeps striving. True faith keeps aiming. True faith keeps fighting. True faith does not let go. True faith is determined. True faith is steadfast. True faith is tenacious. True faith is persistent.

In making life count and maximizing our time on

earth, we must take the brakes off of our endeavors and live life with no limits. We must tear down any and all walls of obstacle. We must remove the margins of restriction. We must quarantine our trepidations. We must not be afraid to take risks. My advice: elevate your expectations. My advice: extend your perimeters. My advice: broaden your horizons. My advice: enlarge your perspectives. My advice: aim higher. My advice: dream bigger. My advice: try harder. My advice: push yourself further. Go to another level of effort and push yourself into a new dimension of possibilities. Do not be a quitter. Be a finisher. Do not settle for average. Strive to excel in all areas of life. It can be done. You can do it!

In life, there is always something more. In life, there is always something greater. We must not limit ourselves. In fact, no one limits us but us. I dare to say: take the limits off and believe in the God who believes in you. I dare to say: believe in your potential. Your only limitations are the ones you put upon yourself. Maximize your potential. Do not standardize your capabilities. Maximize your potential. Do not stereotype your possibilities. Never put a lid on how far you can go. Indeed, "the sky is the limit," and with faith in God you can go even further. With faith, you can see the invisible. With faith, you can anticipate the indescribable. Again, Jesus says, "all things are possible," if we only believe. Tell yourself: "No limits."

Let there be no limits on healing. Let there be no limits on miracles. Let there be no limits on deliverance. Put no limits on God. Activate your faith. In Second Corinthians 5:7 it is written: "We walk by faith and not by sight." Like God, speak those things that are not as though they were. Like God, there is power in our words.

In fact, the Bible says: "Death and life are in the power of the tongue" (Proverbs 18:21). Guard your words. Be careful of what you utter into the atmosphere. Choose your words wisely. Use the creative authority in your words to make life count. Learn how to declare and decree. Learn how to employ your words in your favor.

If you are to live life with no limits, you must tell yourself: "no fear," "no apprehension," "no excuse," and "no limits." Declare and decree greater in your life. Declare and decree greater for your life. Greater for your family. Greater for your finances. Greater for your church. Greater for yourself. Take the limits off and encourage yourself to do it. Take the limits off and propel yourself into it. What are your dreams? What are your aspirations? What are your goals? What is on your bucket list? What hinders you? Who is preventing you? Take the limits off of yourself. Do not live in fear. Live in faith. Believe it. Plan it. Pursue it. Complete it. Nothing is impossible. Live life with no boundaries, with no restrictions, with no constraints—with No limits! Food for thought: "IN THE END...We only regret the chances we didn't take, the relationships we were afraid to have, and the decisions we waited too long to make" (Lewis Carroll). The choice is yours. The decisions are yours to make.

"You and only you are responsible for your life choices and decisions."
Robert Klyosaki

Chapter Four

CHOICES AND DECISIONS

See, I have set before you today life and good, death and evil, [16] in that I command you today to love the LORD your God, to walk in His ways, and to keep His commandments, His statutes, and His judgments, that you may live and multiply; and the LORD your God will bless you in the land which you go to possess. [17] But if your heart turns away so that you do not hear, and are drawn away, and worship other gods and serve them, [18] I announce to you today that you shall surely perish; you shall not prolong *your* days in the land which you cross over the Jordan to go in and possess. [19] I call Heaven and earth as witnesses today against you, *that* I have set before you life and death, blessing and cursing; therefore, choose life, that both you and your descendants may live.

Deuteronomy 30:15-19 NKJV

The terms "choice" and "decision" are oftentimes used interchangeably, which simply means that they are "capable of being put or used in the place of each other." However, there is a slight difference between a *choice* and a *decision*. The word *choice* creates a mental picture of coming to a fork in the road that is split with options of directions to choose from. Choices are opportunities or prospects that are presented to us. Oftentimes we make a choice based on personal beliefs or instincts without any concrete information or facts. A *decision*, on the other hand, is an analytical method we tend to use in order to eliminate options. A decision is a thoughtful, thorough process considering the facts, which may include our past experience. After weighing the opportunities of choices, purging certain options, we choose a direction. In short, we make a decision.

Each day we live we are faced with choices and decisions. From what clothes we wear to what food we eat. From where we go to what we do. From what we spend to what we save. From who we communicate with and who we avoid. Some choices and decisions are minor, but some are major. And depending on what we choose and decide, we either have a good day or a bad day, we either have a good life or a bad life. Life is full of choices. Good choices. Bad choices. Right choices. Wrong choices. Our lives are inundated or besieged frequently with a multiplicity of decisions we must make. And unless we get to the point in life where we become incapable of making logical choices and decisions for ourselves due to a decline or deterioration in our mental faculties and abilities, we must choose and decide for ourselves.

No one else is responsible or accountable for the choices and decisions we make when we are capable of making them for ourselves. No one else has the 'power of attorney' for our choices and decisions when we can make them for ourselves. Yes, life is full of choices and decisions, and every choice and decision has consequences. Every choice and decision has an end result or final outcome. Based on what we choose or decide, we either gain or lose, we either succeed or fail, we either progress or regress, and we either live or die. In the realm of eternity, based on what and who we choose and decide to follow, we will end up in either Heaven or Hell.

As we journey through life, there is no choice or decision more critical than our commitment to God. Our commitment to God is the determining factor between whether or not our lives are blessed or cursed. Our commitment to God is the barometer which gauges the level of our obedience to God and the intensity of our love for God. Based on our commitment to God, we either demonstrate loyalty or infidelity and we either side with God or against Him. There is no middle ground. There is no area of compromise. God expects from those of us who claim Him as LORD a total submission to His Will and a total trust in His Word. Total means: complete, absolute, undivided, and uninterrupted. Total means we are *all in* or in the urban vernacular, we are *sold out*. This means that everything we have belongs to God and all we have is readily available for His purpose. God is looking for individuals who are *sold out* to Him and for Him. Nothing less is acceptable.

In the passage of Deuteronomy 30:15-19, we note that the nation of Israel is on the brink of inheriting the Promised Land of Canaan. However, Moses, who has led the Israelites to this point from bondage to blessing, would not cross over with them. Instead, Moses would soon die. But before his death, Moses outlines the blessings and curses that would occur contingent upon the people's obedience or disobedience to God. Before his death, Moses chronicles the blessings and curses and he calls on the people to make a choice. Either choose *life* or *death*. Life was the choice of God—loving Him and obeying Him. Death was the choice of rejecting God

23

through defiance of His commandments. The blessings of God would come to those who were obedient to God. The curses to those who were disobedient. And the same applies today. What we receive from God is based upon our choices and decisions concerning God. It is just as simple as that!

We all have choices. We all must make decisions. None of us are robots. None of us are puppets on a string. God has endowed each human life with the conscience of free will. Free will is defined as: "the power of acting without the constraint of necessity or fate." It is "the ability to act at one's own discretion" or "the ability to choose between different possible courses of action unimpeded." The concept of free will is closely linked to the concepts of guilt, sin, responsibility, accountability, and other judgments which apply only to actions that are freely chosen. In judgment, God will hold each life responsible for what is chosen freely through free will because each life has the right to choose. Concerning His will, God does not force His will on anyone. God has the authority and ability to do so; however, God will never twist our arms to either love Him or choose Him. These choices and decisions are left up to us.

As it was the choice of the Israelites to obey or disobey God, whether to choose God or not is our choice. The Israelites chose unwisely and suffered the consequences of their ill-advised decision. The Israelites were offered the choice of life (acceptance of God) or death (rejection of God) and that of good (moral living) or evil (immorality). They made the wrong choice. The question is: what choice will the people of God make today? We are given the same offers and the same choices: "Choose life, that both you and your descendants may live" (Deuteronomy 30:19 NKJV). Choose loving God. Choose walking in His ways. Choose keeping God's commandments. Choose doing God's will. Choose to obey God. Choose to reverence (honor) His name. Choose to submit to His sovereignty. Make the choice of God's Son Jesus Christ. In the Bible it is written: "He who has the Son has life; he who does not have the Son of God does not have life" (1 John 5:12 NKJV). It is a simple choice. It is a destiny decision.

The decision to choose Jesus as Lord and Savior is not hard when you factor in God's unconditional and sacrificial love for us. It is not hard when you consider God's never-ending supply of grace. It is not hard when you ponder God's goodness and His mercy. It is not hard when you know that your sins have been forgiven although you are not worthy. It is not hard when you look to Calvary. It is not hard when you behold the crucifixion. It is not hard when you realize it should have been you. It is not hard when you know that Jesus died in your place. The choice becomes easier the more we think about it and the more we look back over our lives. As it is written: "If it had not been the LORD who was on our side" (Psalm 124:1). As for me, my choice of Jesus and decision to acknowledge Him as Lord of my life is the best choice and decision I have made. I cannot speak for anyone else, but for me it is the world behind me and the cross before me. For me, it is 'for God I live and for God I die.' My testimony is summed up in the song, "I Have Decided to Make Jesus My Choice" (Harrison Johnson). What about you?

What is your choice? What is your decision? Is your mind made up? Do you love God wholeheartedly? Let me help you out. "He [Jesus] was wounded for our transgressions, He was bruised for our iniquities: the chastisement of our peace was upon Him, and with His stripes we are healed" (Isaiah 53:5). Let me help you out. "For God so loved the world, that He gave His only begotten Son, that whosoever believeth in Him should not perish, but have everlasting life" (John 3:16). Let me help you out. "But God commendeth His love toward us, in that, while we were yet sinners, Christ died for us" (Romans 5:8). Let me help you out. Nobody will ever love you like God does. God's love for us is absolute. *Absolute* means it is "not qualified or diminished in any way." It means that nothing can be done to prevent God from loving us (all human life). Is there anything that can diminish God's love for us? I stand with the Apostle Paul's declaration: "I am persuaded that neither death, nor life, nor angels, nor principalities, nor powers, nor things present, nor things to come, nor height, nor depth, nor any other creature shall be able to separate us from the love of God, which is in Christ Jesus our Lord" (Romans 8:38-39).

As I stated before: We all have choices. We all must make decisions. None of us are robots and none of us are puppets on a string. We must choose and decide for ourselves whether or not to live life on God's terms. Each life has a choice and each life must make a choice. When it comes to God it is "yes" or "no." There is no middle ground or gray area. Make the choice. You cannot abstain. Make the choice. None of us will get a pass as we stand before the Judgment Seat of God. I leave you with these words: Choose today whom you will serve. If your choice is God and His Son Jesus, you have chosen well. But if not, you will suffer the consequences of snubbing the Creator of all human life and Redeemer of all converted souls. I leave you with these words: "As for me and my house, we will serve the LORD" (Joshua 24:15 NKJV), and "my house" means ME. I cannot choose nor decide for anyone else but myself. You must choose and decide for YOU. Maximize your time on earth by choosing God and His Son Jesus Christ! Maximize your time on earth by traveling down the right road within life!

"When you come to a fork in the road, if you do not know where
you want to go, then it does not matter which road you take.
But take a road you must. Hopefully, it is the right road."
Larry A. Brookins

Chapter Five

THE ROADS WE TRAVEL

There is a way that appears to be right, but in the end, it leads to death.
Proverbs 14:12 NIV

Enter through the narrow gate. For wide is the gate and broad is the road that leads to destruction, and many enter through it. But small is the gate and narrow the road that leads to life, and only a few find it.
Matthew 7:13-14 NIV

You may be familiar with the story of "Alice in Wonderland" (Lewis Carroll). In the mystical realm of Wonderland, the character Alice comes to a split in a road that leads off into different directions. At the split, Alice sees a Cheshire (CHESH-ur *or* CHESH-er) cat and seeks some advice. Her question is: "Would you tell me please, which way I ought to go from here?" The cat's reply is: "That depends a good deal on where you want to get to." Alice says: "I do not much care where I go." The cat responds: "Then it does not matter which way you go." What an interesting dialogue from a beloved children's story. The dialogue between Alice and the Cheshire cat provides us with a moral lesson, which is: "destination is everything."

If we are like Alice where destination does not matter, then any road we travel within life will do. But if we care where we will end up, then we must choose the road (pathway) that will take us where we want to go. Why is the road of choice so important? It is important because our direction of travel is crucial to whether or not we reach our destination. In life, destination is everything. In life, depending upon our destination, the road or roads we choose are fundamental. As we discussed in Chapter Four, the choices we make are critical to the outcomes of our lives. A wrong choice can produce an undesired conclusion, while a right choice can make all the difference in the world. For example: if Heaven is our destination, then we must choose the path that will get us there. We cannot journey in life down a trail of wicked living and expect to end up in Heaven. In this, we only delude ourselves. In this, we only fool ourselves. The roads we travel in life determine our placement on the other side of the grave.

Some religions will say that any road will lead to God. Some even teach that there are many paths that one can take. However, such teaching is contrary to what is written in the Bible. In the Bible, which is viewed as the "Word of God," there is a right road and a wrong road or a right way and a wrong way. In fact, in God's Word there is only one way to ensure that our life's journey leads to Him. It is through His Son Jesus Christ. According to John 14:6, He is the Way, the Truth, and the Life, and no one comes to God except through Him. According to John 10:9, He is the Door. In other words, Jesus is the only access to salvation, abundant life (John 10:10), and eternal life (John 3:16). In John 10:9 Jesus says: "I am THE Door," not A door. A door gives you options. A door implies many possibilities. But there are no options or possibilities besides Jesus adequate enough to supply us with a relationship and fellowship with God. The right choice and only choice is Jesus. The right road and only road that ends in relationship and fellowship with God is Jesus. Let us talk about the roads we travel.

As noted underneath the topic of this chapter, we mention two texts of Scripture: Proverbs 14:12 and Matthew 7:13-14. We will get to the Proverbs text shortly but let me discuss the Matthew text here. In Matthew 7:13-14, Jesus gives a discourse about two gates, two roads, two quantities of travelers, and two conclusions. One gate is described as "narrow," the other "wide." One road is "broad," the other "narrow." Through the wide gate and down the broad road many enter and travel. Through the narrow gate and down the narrow road are just a few people. Why so many travelers down the broad road and why so few travelers down the narrow road?

We live in a society where people are drawn to big crowds. Big crowds give the illusion of excitement, security, comfort, as well as a sense of belonging. Some people like a crowd because it enables them to blend in to either fit in or hide. Others feel they may be missing something if they do not hang out with the crowd. Missing out on a good time. Missing out on enjoyment and pleasure. Missing out on fun and fantasy. Missing out on recreational activity, as well as on life itself. But the truth of the matter is: hanging out in a crowd can pervert one's life. It can corrupt, degrade, debase, and devastate. In First Corinthians 15:33 it is written: "Bad company corrupts good character" (NIV). The truth of the matter is: hanging with a crowd can put us on the wrong path within life. Many good people became and become

31

bad people because of their association with the wrong people. *Association* tends to produce *assimilation*. "Evil influence is like a nicotine patch, you cannot help but absorb what sticks to you" (Quote from "Brushstrokes of a Gadfly," E.A. Bucchianeri). The roads we travel and the people we travel with impact our present environment, as well as our future.

Do not be fooled. A crowd is not always indicative of the place to be. Never get caught up in the "everybody is doing it" thought. The truth of the matter is: regardless of what it is, not everybody is doing it. The truth of the matter is: there is always another crowd. We simply must choose which assembly of people to infiltrate. We simply must choose which road to journey on in life. A crowd followed Adolph Hitler. A crowd followed Jim Jones. A crowd followed David Koresh. A crowd followed Marshall Applewhite. Never go along just to belong. Never give in just to fit in. Proverbs 14:12 states: "There is a way that appears to be right, but in the end, it leads to death" (NIV).

Too many people do things without knowing why. Too many people do things simply because someone else is doing it. People drink for such a reason. People smoke for such a reason. People do drugs for such a reason. People have sex for such a reason. People get tattooed for such a reason. People have babies for such a reason. People join gangs for such a reason. People cuss for such a reason. Ask yourself: "Why do you do what you do?" Why do young men walk around with their pants down? Why do young girls walk around with their skirts up? Like birds in a flock, people follow the pack. But sometimes following the pack can lead to peril. Oftentimes following the pack will lead to peril.

In making life count, we must be careful which gate we walk through, and which road we travel down, and which crowd we hang with, for it makes a difference in life. Beyond this life there are only two destinations: Heaven or Hell. When we leave this earth through death, it is either one or the other. Both are real and both are contingent upon the roads we travel now in life. We cannot afford to play Russian roulette with the destiny of our souls. None of us know when we will leave here. Thus, the question becomes: Where do you want to go? The question becomes: Where do you want to end up? The question is: What road are you on?

If the destination is Heaven, we cannot walk down the road of worldliness doing worldly things. We cannot mix it up and turn it up with worldly people. James 4:4 says: "Friendship with the world is enmity with God" (NKJV). What does this mean? It means we have to choose. We cannot be friends both with the world and with God. Worse yet, anyone who continues to befriend the world lives as enemies of God. This is not to say that, as Christians, we cannot be friends with non-Christians nor that we cannot engage in some of the culture of this world. It is to say we must decide to either live according to the whims of the world or the wisdom of God. The two are diametrically opposed to one another. When at the fork in the road, it is either God or the world. When at the fork in the road, it is either the world's way or God's way. Here is what the Word of God says: "Love not the world, neither the things that are in the world" (1 John 2:15). Here is what the Word of God says: "Come out from among them, and be ye separate, says the Lord, and touch not the unclean thing, and I will receive you" (2 Corinthians 6:17 NKJV).

If Heaven is the destination, then the *right* road is the *righteous* road. The righteous road is the road occupied by people who seek to live for God. By people who love God. By people who trust God. By people who obey God. By people who submit their lives to the will of God. These people are devoted to God. These people are loyal to God. These people are passionate about God. These people are steadfast, unmovable, and always abounding in the work of God. These people are on the righteous road. The righteous road is the least traveled road, but it is the road that leads to life. It is the road that leads to Heaven.

On the righteous road people help one another. On the righteous road people love their enemies. On the righteous road people love their neighbors. On the righteous road people love God. On the righteous road people feed the hungry. On the righteous road people clothe the naked. On the righteous road people visit the sick. On the righteous road people show compassion. The righteous road is the narrow road. Here people forgive each other, and encourage each other, and build up each other, and respect one another. Here people are not perfect, but they strive to live according to God's will. If you are not on this road, it is not too late to switch roads. The choice is yours. The narrow road is not a popular road, but it is the right road. If one day you want to hear God say "well done," leave the crowd and come on over. Leave the glitz and the glamor and come on over.

The broad way has lots of people making lots of noise, but the broad way leads to destruction. Make life count. Do not get trapped. Make life count. Do not get enticed.

Make life count. Do not become ensnared. Make life count. Do not be distracted or detoured. "All that glitters is not gold." It may look good, or sound good, or feel good, but all that looks good, and sounds good, and feels good is not necessarily good. "There is a way that appears to be right" (Proverbs 14:12 NIV). In life, be careful where you travel. In life, be careful with whom you associate. In life, be careful of the temptations around you. In life, do not adopt and adapt to the ways of the world. The instruction from God's Book is: "Do not be conformed to this world, but be transformed by the renewing of your mind, that you may prove what is that good and acceptable and perfect will of God" (Romans 12:2 NKJV).

The roads we travel are critical. They are central to our salvation and destination. If the desired final stop is Heaven, then Jesus says: "Enter through the narrow gate" (Matthew 7:13 NIV). The narrow gate gives way to a narrow road, but it leads to life (Matthew 7:14). It leads to the forgiveness of sins. It leads to the redemption of souls. It leads to God. In making life count and maximizing your time on earth, do not go through the wrong gate. Do not travel the wrong road. Do not hang with the wrong people. Do not partner with this world. Do not go along just to get along. Live your life to please God. Let your testimony be: "For God I live and for God I die" and "the cross before me with the world behind me." No turning back. No turning back.

Remember: there is only one right way, and one right choice, and one right gate, and one right road. The right Way is Jesus. The right Choice is Jesus. The right Gate is Jesus. The right Road is Jesus. Songwriter Thomas Dorsey penned these lyrics: "It's a highway to Heaven;

none can walk up there but the pure in heart. It's a highway to Heaven; I am walking up the King's highway" (It's A Highway to Heaven). The narrow road is the King's highway, and there is joy on the King's highway, and there is peace on the King's highway, and there is deliverance on the King's highway, and there is forgiveness on the King's highway. As you journey in life, make the right choice and choose the right road. The right choice and the right road leads to eternal life. Make the right choice and travel down the right road and make an impact with your life!

"People will forget what you said, people will forget what you did, but people will never forget how you made them feel."
Maya Angelou

Chapter Six

MAKE AN IMPACT

You are the salt of the earth; but if the salt loses its flavor,
how shall it be seasoned? It is then good for nothing but
to be thrown out and trampled underfoot by men.
Matthew 5:13 NKJV

Matthew 5:13 is part of an extensive teaching communicated by Jesus to a multitude of people on a hillside in Galilee (Matthew 5:1-2). This extensive teaching is aptly called "The Sermon on the Mount." It takes place in the early stages of Jesus' ministry shortly after Jesus' baptism in the Jordan River by John the Baptist, and shortly after His 40 day and night temptation experience in the wilderness, and shortly after His selection of His first twelve disciples. In this discourse by Jesus, He calls attention to the type of routine and character that should be present in the lives of His followers. In this discourse by Jesus, He lays the groundwork for a new kingdom whose citizens are to be committed to a new lifestyle. This new lifestyle must be lived in accordance with God's commandments and exemplary of Jesus Christ. In this new lifestyle, everything that is said or done should measure up to the expectations of Jesus. In this new lifestyle, the follower of Jesus should demonstrate his or her newfound belief in Jesus as Christ, Son of God and Savior of the world. In this new lifestyle, whatever we do should impact the world around us in such a way that what is done brings glory to God.

No life should be lived, especially the Christian life, without purpose or influence. The Christian lifestyle should sway the lives of others toward Christ and impact the lives of others for the better. From Chapter 5 through Chapter 7 of the Book of Matthew we are given instruction on how to live, and on how to conduct ourselves, and on how to interact with others, and on how to make an impact in this world for the Kingdom of God. From Chapter 5 through Chapter 7 Jesus covers a multiplicity of topics, all designed to impart the standards of God for His people and all intended to impart the importance of everyday life and how critical it is that life is not wasted through futility, or insignificance, or ineffectiveness. It is this point of value, efficiency, and ability to affect that is central to the metaphor used by Jesus in identifying His followers as "the salt of the earth."

In His depiction of His followers as "salt," Jesus uses a familiar substance to drive home the idea of influence or impact. In first century Palestine "salt" was used to preserve and flavor food, as well as for the purpose of healing. As a preservative; salt serves as a sponge, soaking up and eliminating water from food, thereby, making food too dry to support unsafe mold or bacteria. Mold and bacteria need moisture and with moisture, mold and bacteria decays and can cause disease or virus. Both mold and bacteria are destroyed by a high concentration of salt. Salt kills germs and salt can expedite the mending of open wounds. As flavoring, salt gives food taste. Despite the fact that too much salt in our food can be harmful, salt is good for us. Without salt, we would die from what is called "hyponatremia." Hyponatremia is defined as "a low sodium level in the blood." "Sodium," or "sodium chloride" (NaCl), is the scientific name for "salt." In order to survive, we need salt.

The minerals in salt supply our bodies with electrolytes. "Electrolytes" are nutrients that are needed within our bodies to enable our bodies to function as they should. Their function ranges from regulating our heartbeat to allowing our muscles to contract so we can move. The major electrolytes within our bodies are: calcium, magnesium, potassium, phosphate, chloride, and sodium. Again, *sodium* is *salt*. Salt helps with fluid balance and salt helps with nerve transmission. We need salt. However, like anything else that tastes good to us or is good for us, it can become easy to consume too much salt. Although salt is good for us, we have to be careful of how much we intake, especially if we have health issues such as: high blood pressure or kidney problems. A healthy kidney will extract and excrete salt in excess of what we need, but if the kidney is bad, we must monitor the amount of salt we ingest. Salt adds flavor. Salt enhances taste. Salt preserves and salt purifies, but salt, especially "sea salt," also heals.

Pure sea salt is natural and the use of sea salt can alleviate ailments caused by arthritis, eczema, inflammation, rheumatism, and psoriasis. Also, a pinch of salt sprinkled on the tongue may help to improve allergic reactions and or asthma attacks. It has also been said that salt improves sleep quality. Salt can also remove dead skin cells and relieve muscular tension. In so many ways, salt is essential for life and we cannot exist without it. In so many ways, salt is beneficial to us and for us and salt complements our lives more so than detracts from our lives. For these reasons Jesus employs salt to equate the Christian life. As Christians, we are called "the salt of the earth" because our lives, like salt, should enhance and supplement. As Christians, like salt, we should impact what we contact. Like salt, we should add flavor and preservation. Like salt, we should bring value to the world. With lives that are lived to please God, we should slow the decay of morality and holiness. By living a Christlike life, we should showcase to the world "what is that good and acceptable and perfect will of God" (Romans 12:2 NKJV). In the world, as salt, we should be a benefit and not a detriment. In the world, as salt, we should be influential and instrumental. Someone with influence is someone who affects how things are done and how people live. Someone with influence is someone who is a game changer, a difference maker, a reservoir of resource, and someone who has a significant impact on others.

As Christians, if we make no difference with our lives we serve no purpose. As Christians, if we improve nothing, we become as useless as salt that has lost its ability to augment (boost) what it touches. In this, we are warned. Jesus says, "if salt loses its flavor, how shall it be seasoned again? It is then good for nothing but to be trampled underfoot by men" (Matthew 5:13). Good for nothing! I am just saying what Jesus said. As followers of Christ, we are "the salt of the earth," but if we compromise our beliefs, and if we concede our standards, and if we camouflage our discipleship, and if we veil our light, then we dilute our declarations and we undermine our testimonies. In this, we become ineffective ambassadors for Christ. In this, we drain the potency of our witness as Christians. We waste our efforts. We squander opportunities. We misrepresent who we say we are. We make no impact for the Kingdom of God.

If we make no impact for God's Kingdom, why then are we here? If we make no impact for God's Kingdom, why then do we claim Jesus as Lord and Savior? In essence, we perpetrate falsehood. In essence, we devalue our relevance. What good is salt if it cannot season? What good is salt if it has no strength? The point that Jesus makes is: we have a high and holy calling as Christians. The point that Jesus makes is: as Kingdom citizens we must make a Kingdom impact. In other words, we must do what we can to make the world a better place. In other words, we must do what we can to purge the world of sin. We are "the salt of the earth." As salt, where there is strife, we must be peacemakers. As salt, where there is sorrow, we must be comforters. As salt, where there is hurt, we must be healers. As salt, where there is hate, we must be love. As salt, where there is need, we must supply. As salt, where there is weakness, we must strengthen. As salt, where there is trouble, we must help. As salt, where there is fault, we must forgive. We are "the salt of the earth."

As Christians, it is up to us to make a difference. As Christians, it is up to us to make an impact. We must do something to preserve. We must do something to purify. We must do something to enhance. We must do something to influence. We are the agents of change. We are God's instruments of transformation. We represent the Kingdom. We represent the Church. We represent the Christian Faith. We represent Jesus Christ. If not us, then who? As the "salt of the earth," we must be symbols of grace. As the "salt of the earth," we must be symbols of mercy. As the "salt of the earth," we must be symbols of virtue. As the "salt of the earth," we must be symbols of godliness. One more time: we are "the salt of the earth."

As salt, we make our lives count when we share. As salt, we make our lives count when we care. As salt, we make our lives count when we give. As salt, we make our lives count when we pour our lives into others. As salt, we make an impact when we lift up each other. As salt, we make an impact when we serve one another. As salt, we make an impact when we turn the other cheek. As salt, we make an impact when we go the extra mile. When we feed the hungry, we make an impact. When we clothe the naked, we make an impact. When we house the homeless, we make an impact. When we visit the sick, we make an impact. This is what Jesus instructs us to do. This is what, as Christians, we ought to do. We ought to make an impact. We ought to flavor our community. We ought to flavor our church. We ought to flavor our home. We ought to flavor our environment.

If our lives are to count as Christians, we need to spice things up and make things better. We need to improve what we touch. We need to impact every contact. We need to make an impact with our words. We need to make an impact with our deeds. We need to make an impact with our character. We need to make an impact with our life. We must live for God. We must set the right example. We must replicate the mind of Jesus Christ. We must live holy as instructed in God's Word (1 Peter 1:16). Do not let your living be in vain. Make an impact. Do not let your spiritual rebirth be pointless. Make an impact. Maximize your time on earth. Be effective. Maximize your time on earth. Be relevant. Maximize your time on earth. Be useful. Maximize your time on earth. Be productive. Disinfect. Maintain. Engage. Modify. We are "the salt of the earth." It is up to us to make a difference. Mahalia Jackson sang, "If I can help somebody as I pass along, if I can cheer somebody with a word or song, if I can show somebody that he's traveling wrong, then my living shall not be in vain. If I can do my duty as a Christian ought, if I can bring back beauty to a world up wrought, if I can spread love's message as the Master taught, then my living shall not be in vain. My living shall not be in vain, then my living shall not be in vain. If I can help somebody as I pass along, then my living shall not be in vain" (If I Can Help Somebody). Make your life count. Make an impact!

"Focus on today. Do not allow what happened yesterday
to disturb today. Leave the past in the past."
Larry A. Brookins

Chapter Seven

DO NOT DWELL ON THE PAST

Forget the former things; do not dwell on the past.

Isaiah 43:18 NIV

Every year comes to a close; however, some people find it difficult to let go of what has been in favor of embracing what is to come. Every year gives way to a new year and with a new year comes the opportunity to move on from the episodes of a year that is headed for the archives of history. Every person has a past, present, and future, but some people cannot embrace their present nor plan their future because they are stuck in their past.

Too many people are stuck in the past looking at the still frames of life when in reality time is constantly moving and flowing. We are all time travelers. If we are to fully realize God's purpose and destiny for our life and to get the great things God wants for us, we are to keep moving in the flow of life. In other words, do not live in the past! The *past* is defined as: "gone by in time and no longer existing." It is any period of time before the present. Too many people fail to maximize their time on earth and live the life God created us to experience because they refuse to bid farewell to yesterday or to yesteryear. While it is alright to remember the past, when remembrance of the past encumbers the possibilities of life we must write our past an obituary and entomb its events in antiquity.

Why is it important to keep moving forward? It is important because time wasted dwelling in the past robs us of living life to its fullest. Moreover, when we are handcuff to our past, we fail to seize the power of every moment and we miss out on enjoying the great future God has prepared for us. It is also important because we can only progress forward when we stop looking in the rear-view mirror of life. God never intended for us to keep reliving moments in our past—past relationships, past jobs, past successes, and past failures.

From God's perspective, our future is far more important than our past. In other words, where we are going is more important than where we have been. This is why a car has a large windshield so we can see where we are going. This is why a car has a small rear-view mirror to limit the time we spend looking backwards. "You can't drive forward by looking in the rear-view mirror" (T.D. Jakes). Dwelling or living in the past can even shorten your life. The biblical story of Lot's wife demonstrates how dangerous it is to live life looking backwards. After being warned not to look behind her, Lot's wife became a pillar of salt after she looked back at the destruction of Sodom (Genesis 19:17-26). We all need to "Remember Lot's wife" (Luke 17:32).

Dwelling on the past is also like dragging old baggage into a new year; it delays and prevents our forward movement. What is *old baggage*? Old baggage is the stuff we tend to carry around from our past including life experiences that are not so pleasant to or for us. It is the stuff that burdens our heart every time we reflect on it.

It is the stuff that makes us sad, frustrated, angry and depressed every time we think about it. It is stuff that emotionally drains us. It is stuff that leaves us fixed to our past feeling sorry for ourselves. It is stuff that depletes us of the will to embrace life. It is stuff that prevents us from looking ahead or trying again. We all have baggage.

Baggage is a part of life. Each one of us is shaped by encounters and occurrences from our lives—the good, the bad, and the ugly. Nobody journeys through life unscathed. Just ask Joseph and Job. Everybody endures some form of hurt baggage, heartache baggage, incident baggage, and accident baggage. However, the key to moving forward is to let go of every piece of annoying or repulsive baggage. As God's Word reminds us: the best way to move forward is to lay aside all burdensome baggage that weighs us down and decelerates our advancement (Hebrews 12:1).

While every life has a past, God does not want us to dwell on the past. *Dwell* means: "to live in or at a specified place." When we dwell somewhere, we remain there for a time. When we dwell somewhere, we give that place our attention, fixation, or obsession. The problem with dwelling on the past is that we lock ourselves to the past. The problem with dwelling on the past is that we cease to live in the present and we negate the opportunities of tomorrow. When we dwell on the past, we get stuck. When we dwell on the past, we sabotage our potential. When we dwell on the past, we undermine our future. When we dwell on the past, we endanger our health. Dwelling on the past can make us sick with worry, sorrow, confusion, and depression.

Unlike dwelling, glancing at the past is not always a

bad thing. A *glance* is "a brief or hurried look." When we glance at the past, we quickly learn the lessons it teaches and we move on. This means we do not keep pondering what could have been or thinking about what should have been. This means we do not ponder about the what ifs of our past. Instead, we simply glean what we can from the past and leave the negative and useless baggage of the past behind. The past is the past. We must live in the moment. We cannot change the past. We can make amends, but we cannot undo what has been done. What is the reality? The reality is: what is in the past is over. The reality is: what is in the past has ended. It is gone and we need to move on. Isaiah 43:18 says: "Forget the former things; do not dwell on the past" (NIV).

One thing that will help us in releasing the past is reciting the words of *The Serenity Prayer*: "God grant me the SERENITY to accept the things I cannot change, COURAGE to change the things I can, and WISDOM to know the difference" (Reinhold Niebuhr). In order to progress, we must know the difference between what we cannot change and what we can. One undisputable fact is that we cannot change the past. We can, however, change our future. How do we know it is time to move forward into our future?

- If a relationship has soured and you are no longer wanted, move on.
- If your job lets you go, move on.
- When people leave your life, move on.
- When the memory is too painful, move on.

Despite the fact that moving on is difficult and even painful, we must:

- Seek something new.
- Start something new.
- Get some help.
- Learn how to let go.

In other words, in order to keep moving forward we must not dwell on the past!

Dwelling on the past keeps us in a dark place and it can destroy our lives. It can depress us. It can paralyze us. It can abort our aspirations. It can stunt our growth. If we made a mistake, we made a mistake. Everybody makes mistakes. God's Word instructs us to confess our mistakes (sins) to Him (1 John 1:9), ask God for forgiveness, forgive ourselves and move on. None of us are perfect. No one is flawless. The reality is: all will fall and make mistakes in this life. The Word of God declares it (Romans 3:23). Thank God that He does not give up on us when we mess up. God is not shackled by our actions or inactions. God can use anyone (saint or sinner) who avails themselves to be used of Him. We cannot allow our mistakes of the past to keep us in a holding pattern for the rest of our lives. Once we admit that we have messed up, God will forgive us (1 John 1:9).

God wants to continuously write new chapters in the book of our lives. However, new chapters are not possible if we keep re-visiting old chapters. My advice: leave the past in the past. Do not drag baggage from one year to the next. We cannot start a new chapter if we keep re-reading previous chapters. My advice: give the last chapter of your life closure. Do not dwell on the past and do not define yourself by your past. Do not fetter yourself to your past. Do not keep gazing back at your past. Close the door on the past. Close the door and do not loiter or linger. Shut the door, lock it, and throw the key away. It may be difficult to forget, but dwelling makes it worst. It may be problematic to ignore, but dwelling makes it worst. From your work life to your love life, do not give your past the victory of overshadowing your present nor let it prevent you from having the future that God wants you to have. This is what His Word says: "For I know the plans I have for you," declares the LORD, "plans to prosper you and not to harm you, plans to give you hope and a future" (Jeremiah 29:11).

No matter what happens in our lives, life goes on. It will go on with or without us. How it goes on with us is up to us. Failure is not final. The past is not the end. We should use our past for reference, not residence. Do not let your past hold you hostage or cancel your future. Look ahead and plan ahead. Realign your thoughts and reorder your steps. Again, Isaiah 43:18 says: "Forget the former things; do not dwell on the past" (NIV). It is time for a fresh start. It is time for a new beginning. Shake off the dust of past disappointment. Shake off the dust of past rejection. Shake off the dust of past confusion. Shake off the dust of past failure. Shake off the dust of brokenness. Shake off the dust of loss. Shake off the dust of heartbreak. Shake off the dust of resentment. Make life count and believe God's plans for your life. Do not dwell on the past.

If you are holding on to anything, let it go. Whatever you are holding on to, let it go. If something is preventing you from moving forward, even if the *something* is a *someone*, let it go. Do not give the past power over your present, let it go. Move on! Go forward! Let bygones be bygones! Let the past stay the past! Here we go. Countdown to a new you: ten, nine, eight, seven, six, five, four, three, two, one. Do not look back. Do not go back. Shut the door and lock it and throw the key away. Decree to yourself: It is a new season for my life. Decree to yourself: old things are old things. I will not resuscitate my past. Bid your past *goodbye* so you can tell your present and your future *hello*. Make life count. Maximize your time on earth. Do not dwell on the past! The sun is shining today. Enjoy it. Embrace your new day with a new you. Stop dwelling on the past!

"You may delay, but time will not, and lost time is never found again."
Benjamin Franklin

Chapter Eight

THE POISON OF PROCRASTINATION

Don't put it off; do it now! Don't rest until you do.
Proverbs 6:4 NLT

From the wisdom Book of Proverbs, we are given a nugget of priceless advice: "Don't put it off; do it now! Don't rest until you do" (NLT). Putting things off is the definition of "procrastination." Procrastination is a toxic behavior that delays progress and if it is allowed to persist, it can abort or terminate altogether any desire or plan of improvement, or advancement, or implementation, or aspiration. Procrastination is an adversary of accomplishment. Procrastination is an inhibitor of intention. Procrastination is a goal blocker. Procrastination is a dream killer. It is a vision frustrater and a poison that penetrates and intercepts the ideas of our minds and the ambitions of our lives. Anything that is poisonous is destructive. Anything that is poisonous is harmful. Poison impairs and poison corrodes. Poison contaminates and poison assassinates. These are the side effects of procrastination.

One of the biggest ravagers of our days is procrastination. We waste a lot of time suspending things or postponing activity to another time or day. Oftentimes, in actuality, in the present time or day, we have the time to make it happen. However, we say: "I will do it tomorrow." However, we say: "I will get to it later." But when later comes, nothing happens. But when tomorrow arrives, the deferments of yesterday become the deferments of today. In essence, what could have been done still goes undone. The "day" becomes a week, and the "week" becomes a month, and the "month" becomes a year, and the "years" roll on until we grow old and eventually die with unfinished business. Here is a quote worth pondering: "Procrastination is, hands down, our favorite form of self-sabotage" (Alyce P. Cornyn-Selby). What is meant by the term "self-sabotage?" *Self-sabotage* is defined as: "behavior that creates problems and conduct that interferes with long-standing goals." Examples are: self-medication with drugs or alcohol, comfort eating, and various other forms of self-injury. But the most self-sabotaging behavior or conduct is procrastination.

To a greater or lesser degree, we all procrastinate. To a greater or lesser degree, we all are guilty of giving certain activities within our days and lives a rain check. We are all guilty of putting things off. We are all guilty of delaying things until later. We are all guilty of stalling activity. We are all guilty of rescheduling plans and appointments. On one end, there is nothing wrong with rescheduling things when more pressing matters arise. On one end, there is nothing wrong with rearranging things when something comes up that requires our immediate attention. However, we ought not to reschedule or rearrange things and not revisit or restart what we have stopped. This is a symptom of procrastination. This is characteristic of the procrastinator. Are you a procrastinator? You might just be. If you constantly start something but never finish, you may be infected. If you frequently put things on pause but never resume what you have paused, you may be infected. If you persistently prolong things until the last minute, you may be infected. If you habitually make excuses why you cannot do something, you may be infected. Infected with what? Infected with the poison of procrastination.

There are many reasons why people procrastinate. There are many reasons why people drag their feet on responsibilities or on the desires of their heart. Some people have extenuating circumstances. Some people are overwhelmed with multiple responsibilities. Some people get distracted along the way. Some people are simply lazy. Take a moment and ask yourself: "What is my category?" One of the principal components of procrastination is laziness. On the subject of *laziness*, the Bible has a lot to say. "Lazy hands make a man poor" (Proverbs 10:4 NIV). "Lazy people want much but get little" (Proverbs 13:4 NLT). "A lazy person is as bad as someone who destroys things" (Proverbs 18:9 NLT). "Despite their desires, the lazy will come to ruin, for their hands refuse to work" (Proverbs 21:25 NLT). Refusing to work is indicative of laziness. Sleeping too much is symptomatic of a slothful spirit. *Slothful* means *lazy*. In the King James Version of the Bible, the terms "slothful" and "sluggish" are synonymous with lazy. Proverbs 6:6: "Go to the ant, thou sluggard; consider her ways, and be wise" (Proverbs 6:6). "The hand of the diligent will rule, while the slothful will be put to forced labor" (Proverbs 12:24 ESV).

As human beings, we need sleep. As human beings, sleep is important. However, too much sleep can make us lazy. Too much sleep creates an environment of futility and deficiency. *Futility* is a state of fruitlessness or unprofitability. *Deficiency* is "a lack or shortage" or "a failing or shortcoming." Proverbs 20:13 declares: "Love not sleep, lest you come to poverty; open your eyes, and you will have plenty of bread" (ESV). What is the point? The point is: do not sleep too much. If you are looking for work: do not sleep too much. If you have work to do: do not sleep too much. If you have an appointment to meet: do not sleep too much. If you say that you are not lazy: do not sleep too much. The point is: do not be like *Rip Van Winkle,* going to sleep and waking up 20 years later. Can we talk about the poison of procrastination?

Throughout life, the more we put off, the more we procrastinate. Throughout life, the more we procrastinate, the more disappointment we experience. Procrastination breeds discontent. Procrastination proliferates desolation. If we do nothing, we achieve nothing. If we fail to follow through, we fail to fulfill. If we never finish a book, we will never know the total story. If we never complete a task, we will never feel the satisfaction that is attached to consummation. *Consummation* is "the point at which something is complete or finalized." As we seek to make life count and maximize our time on earth, we must consider the fact that time is valuable and life is short. Once time has passed, we never get it back. Once life nears its end, there are no do-overs. As I state in the introduction, with every tick-tock of the clock, we lose precious moments.

With every movement of the pendulum, the opportunities we have diminish. Therefore, what we plan to do, we should do it. Therefore, when we plan to do it, we ought not to delay.

Tomorrow is not promised to any of us. We have no guarantees of a second chance. With no promise of tomorrow or guarantee of a second chance, we should not allow our work to go undone and we should not waste our days or life. The message is: get it done. The message is: if we do not get it done, it may not get done. The message is: if not now, then when? The late Spanish painter, sculptor, printmaker, ceramicist, stage designer, poet and playwright Pablo Picasso once said: "Only put off until tomorrow what you are willing to die having left undone." Procrastination is our enemy. Procrastinating is a problem. What is the problem? Procrastinating hinders. Procrastinating exasperates. Procrastinating diverts. Procrastinating discontinues. Procrastination is a friend of inactivity and a colleague of discontent. The message is: nip procrastination in the bud. The message is: do not make procrastination a lifestyle.

If you take a break from something, do not break too long, get back on task. Go back to school. Reenter the workforce. Clear the dust off of your dreams and goals. Go back to doing ministry and mission work. Whatever you stopped, start again. Whatever you put on the shelf, take it off. What is hindering you? What are you waiting on? It is detrimental to procrastinate. It is a risky endeavor to postpone. It is decision time. What will you do? I say: make life count. I say: maximize your earthly time. Do not drink the poison of procrastination. Do not delay in accomplishing what you set out to do.

Write that book. Record that song. Open that business. Step out in faith. Finish what you started. Complete what you began. It is decision time. You can do it. It can be done. The moment is now. Make it happen now! You have waited long enough. You have deferred for far too long. Let this be your season. The opportunities are endless. Do not put it off any longer. Do it now! Do not rest until you do. Do not stop until it is done. Make your life count. Maximize your time here on earth by utilizing time to its fullest. Can you hear the sound of the clock? Tick-tock, tick-tock. Tick-tock, tick-tock. Do not procrastinate. Make it happen NOW!

"So it is: we are not given a short life but we make it short,
and we are not ill-supplied but wasteful of it."
Seneca

Chapter Nine

THE COST OF PRODIGAL LIVING

Then He said: A certain man had two sons. And the younger of them said to his father, 'Father, give me the portion of goods that falls to me.' So he divided to them his livelihood. And not many days after, the younger son gathered all together, journeyed to a far country, and there wasted his possessions with prodigal living. But when he had spent all, there arose a severe famine in that land, and he began to be in want. Then he went and joined himself to a citizen of that country, and he sent him into his fields to feed swine. And he would gladly have filled his stomach with the pods that the swine ate, and no one gave him anything.
Luke 15:11-16 NKJV

The story of Luke 15:11-16 is part of a trilogy of stories spoken by Jesus within Chapter 15. These series or cycles of stories are shared in order to underscore or give emphasis to the value of every human life in the sight and heart of God. In the sight and heart of God, every life has value. In the sight and heart of God, every life is worth saving. All three stories of Luke 15 are communicated in response to criticism that Jesus received from religious leaders. These religious leaders complained about the type of people Jesus welcomed in His company and those with whom Jesus ate meals with. In the religious leaders' viewpoint, those whom Jesus welcomed around Him and ate with were despicable sinners unworthy of association. In their viewpoint, these people were repulsive lawbreakers undeserving of attention. How dare Jesus entertain or socialize with these people? How dare Jesus spend time and mingle with these people? Why would Jesus do it? Why did Jesus do it?

Jesus surrounded Himself with individuals who were labeled as the worst of the worst because these were the people He came to earth for and these were the people He eventually would give His life to save. Hear what Jesus says on the matter: "It is not the healthy who need a doctor, but the sick. I have not come to call the righteous, but sinners" (Mark 2:17 NIV). Hear what Jesus says on the matter: "I am not sent but unto the lost sheep of the house of Israel" (Matthew 15:24) and "the Son of man has come to save that which was lost" (Matthew 18:11). The people who were detested by the religious elite were the very ones for whom God sent His Son Jesus to redeem. John 3:17 declares: "For God sent not His Son into the world to condemn the world; but that the world through Him might be saved." Jesus came to salvage lives. Jesus came to give people hope and a second chance at life.

The story of Luke 15:11-16 is the final story of the three redemptive stories of Luke 15. It is a tale of a father with two sons. It is a tale of a loving father who is rich and of his youngest son who wanted to leave his father's house and live life his own way. The youngest son wanted to leave and live life his own way, but with his father's money. The youngest son wanted to leave and live life his own way, but with the funds that his father had earmarked as an inheritance for both of his sons. Generally, an inheritance is passed on from one person to another upon the death of the benefactor. Oftentimes people bequest money, or property, or personal possessions. In the story of Luke 15, we read of a son who could not wait for his father's death. He wanted his share of the inheritance while his father was yet alive. In the story the youngest son approaches his father with an unusual request: "Give me the portion of goods that falls to me" (v. 12). In other words, whatever you plan on leaving me when you die I will take it now, and this is what the father does. Why the father did it we are not informed. How much the youngest son was given we are also not informed. But whatever the amount, not many days after he was given it, the youngest son packed his belongings and left his father's house, going as far away as he could.

With his inheritance, verse 13 of Luke 15 informs us that the youngest son "wasted his possessions with prodigal living" (NKJV). The term *wasted* implies that the youngest son expended all that he had in a careless and foolish manner. Once he left his father's house with his father's inheritance this son, like so many young people do, lived an unrestrained life. Like so many young people do, he lived a loose life, or a wild life, or a self-indulgent life, or a life that was filled with the sort of activities that tends to spiral a life downward into an abyss of wickedness, depravity, debauchery, and deficiency. Perhaps a life of alcohol abuse. Perhaps a life of extreme drug use. Perhaps a life of sexual immortality. Perhaps a life of sinfulness. This is the trademark of prodigal living. *Prodigal living* is a lifestyle of irresponsibility, impulsive conduct, self-destructive behavior, and uncontrolled activities and addictions.

Prodigal is defined as: "a person who spends money or uses his or her resources with wasteful extravagance." This type of person lives life without any thought of consequence or future. This type of person lives recklessly, raucously, imprudently, and indiscreetly. *Indiscreetly* means something is done or said publicly that ought not to be done or said publicly. Indiscreet people lack tact. Indiscreet people lack good judgment. Indiscreet people lack sensitivity. Indiscreet people lack maturity. A lack of tact, good judgment, sensitivity, and maturity are characteristic traits of someone who is prodigal. A prodigal person is a squanderer of money, time, property, and life itself. A person who is prodigal is prone to extravagant spending and partying. Every day is *Mardi Gras* with a prodigal person. Every day is *Fat Tuesday* with a prodigal person. For someone who is prodigal, every day becomes a day of irrational behavior. What is the problem with prodigal living?

Many lives are ruined because of prodigal living. Many homes are shattered because of prodigal living. Many friendships are severed because of prodigal living. Many bank accounts are depleted because of prodigal living. Prodigal living is destructive living. Prodigal living is detrimental living. Prodigal living is toxic living. Prodigal living is disengaging living. It separates. It aborts. It decays. It drains. Living life in a worldly way has repercussions that are costly. Concerning this the Bible is clear: "There is a way which seemeth right unto a man, but the end thereof are the ways of death" (Proverbs 14:12). Do not be fooled. "All that glitters is not gold." Everything that looks good is not necessarily good. Everything that tastes good is not necessarily good. Everything that sounds good is not necessarily good. Everything that feels good is not necessarily good. Do not be fooled. Smoking is hazardous. Alcohol is no joy juice. Promiscuity is idiotic. Sleeping with as many people as you can and as often as you can breeds disease. It will also incur the judgment of God.

Prodigal living is costly. Prostitution is costly. Gang-banging is costly. Drug dealing is costly. Drug use is costly. Do not allow yourself to be hoodwinked by the bright lights of this world nor become enthralled by the alluring billboards lit up along the way. Read the fine print. Sinful living is costly. Read the fine print. The price-tag is too high. The Bible is right: "the wages of sin is death" (Romans 6:23). The Bible is right: "The soul who sins shall die" (Ezekiel 18:4 NKJV). The message: it pays to live for God. The message: It pays to stick with God. Living life contrary to the will of God is not cheap. The cost of prodigal living is the cost of relationship, fellowship, comfort, as well as health and wealth. Prodigal living can cost you the loss of family. Prodigal living can cost you the loss of finances. Prodigal living can cost you the loss of physical fitness. Prodigal living can cost you the loss of your life. Beware! Sin is seductive. Beware! Sin is deceitful. Beware! Sin is devastating. Beware! Sin is highly priced.

Prodigal living is expensive, uneconomical, careless, and wasteful. If you want to make life count, do not waste life with prodigal living. It can ruin your life. If you ever get caught up in it, get out, let it go, make a U-turn, leave it alone. One major lesson of the story of Luke 15 is that it is not too late to come home. However, like the prodigal son of our story, you must come to yourself and make up your mind to make your way back to God. Here is the grace message within the story: God is waiting on your return. Here is the grace message within the story: God is waiting on your recovery. Like the father of the story, God is waiting to redeem you and God is waiting to restore you. His arms are wide-open. His hands are outstretched. His eyes are on the lookout. His forgiveness is on-call. Make life count. If you need God, He is available. Make life count. If you want God, you can have God. God loves us all, no matter how far we have strayed from His presence. If you are living in a prodigal state, Jesus came to earth to bring you home. Come on home!

Maximize your time on earth. The Word is: "Come out from among them" (2 Corinthians 6:17). Come out from loose living. Come out from wild living. Come out from debased behavior. Come out from recklessness. You have sown enough wild oats, done enough sinful things, ingested enough pollution, and wasted enough life. It is time to turn it around. It is time to live right. It is time to live holy. It is time to live wisely. It is time to live for God. Time out for foolishness, stupidity, and waywardness. These are enemies of abundant living. Do not lose your sanity or salvation living a prodigal life. Do not lose the blessings you inherited from God living a prodigal life. Let me say one more time: read the fine print. Prodigal living is reckless, dangerous, foolish, and wasteful. Hear the words of Jesus: "The thief comes only to steal and kill and destroy; I have come that they may have life and have it to the full" (John 10:10 NIV).

Maximize your time on earth. Do not waste it with prodigal living. Make your life count. Live holy. Make your life count. Live a righteous life. Make life count. Live discreetly. Make life count. Live prudently. Do not allow the world to make a fool of you. Do not let the world rob you of precious time or life. Do not let the world leave you broke, busted, and disgusted. Do not let the world suck you in so it can drain you out. One last time: live holy, live righteously, live discreetly, live wisely. Make the most of your earthly journey. Choose God. Stay with God. Never abandon God for worldly living. The cost is simply too high!

""Don't put off living to next week, next month, next year or next decade. The only time you're ever living is in this moment."
Celestine Chua

Chapter Ten

MAKE THE MOST OF TIME

Try to find out what is pleasing to the Lord. Take no part in the
unfruitful works of darkness, but instead expose them. For it
is shameful even to mention what such people do secretly; but
everything exposed by the light becomes visible, for everything
that becomes visible is light. Therefore, it says, "Sleeper,
awake! Rise from the dead, and Christ will shine on you." Be
careful then how you live, not as unwise people but as wise,
making the most of the time, because the days are evil. So do
not be foolish but understand what the will of the Lord is.
Ephesians 5:10-17 NRSV

Whether we realize it or not, we only have a limited
time here on earth. We are told in the Bible that "Life
is but a vapor" (James 4:14), which means: "life is brief"
or "life is transient." Brief and transient simply means:
"Lasting only for a short time." Like a morning mist
that soon vanishes away, our time on earth is short
and its duration is uncertain. We have no guarantees
about the length of our days. We have no guarantees of
time beyond the present moment. We may be young and
healthy, but even age and fitness does not assure us that
our existence will be long. Even if it is long, the question
remains: "how long is long?"

In Psalm 90, Moses weeps over the brevity of life. Though he would live 120 years (Deuteronomy 34:7), Moses compares life to the grass of the field that sprouts in the morning and by evening, it has faded under the hot sun. In verse 10 of Psalm 90 he writes: "As for the days of our life, they contain seventy years, or if due to strength, eighty years, yet their pride is but labor and sorrow; for soon it is gone and we fly away" (NASB). Even if we live as long as Moses lived, how quickly time flies. Someone said, "Life is like the roll of toilet paper—the closer you get to the end, the quicker it goes" (author unknown). We may not care for the analogy, but it is true. Time passes swiftly. Before we know it and if we are blessed to achieve it, one day we will say as David said: "I was young and now I am old" (Psalm 37:25 CEB).

Time is a gift. It is a precious commodity that we should cherish. We should cherish every second of time. We should cherish every minute of time. We should cherish every hour of time. We should cherish every day of time. But not only should we cherish the time that we are endowed with by God, we should also make the most of what time we have. In other words, we should manage our time wisely, and as Christians, we should administer our time in such a way that with our time here on earth, God is pleased. As Christians, we ought not to apportion our time as the world does, squandering time carelessly on things that are only temporal and on things which bring no glory to God. To the contrary, as Christians, we should utilize our time to the benefit of God's will.

Despite the excuses we make, God gives each of us enough time to carry out His will. If we do not, it is not because we do not have the time, but because we fail to prioritize the things of God appropriately with our time. Many times, too many of us place God's will on the back burner of life. We spend our years indulging self in seeking fame, and in seeking fortune, and in seeking fabrics, and in seeking foolishness. Like the prodigal son in Luke Chapter 15, too many of us go through life utilizing the blessings of God on self-destructive activities. Like the prodigal son, we waste too much of life getting drunk, and getting high, and getting laid, and consuming our resources on impulsive behavior. Then, like the prodigal son, we end up broke. We may work and earn wages, but too many of us simply gamble away what we earn. If we get out of bed, some of us only get out of bed to eat, watch TV, and play video games. What a Life. Worse yet, what a waste of life.

Time should be productive. Wasted time is irretrievable. Once time has moved on, it cannot be rewound. In other words, although we can adjust our clocks and watches, we cannot have again the stretch of time that has passed. Once time is gone, it is gone. This is why we cannot afford to procrastinate or delay. It is later than we think. We should seize every moment. It is later than we think. We should capture every chance. It is later than we think. We should occupy every space. It is later than we think. We should make the most of time. If we do not, we limit our life possibilities. If we do not, we can miss out on opportunities that only come once, or not too often in our lifetime. Within our lifetime, we should not have intervals of time with nothing to show for such time. Within our lifetime, there ought not to be long gaps of inactivity or long gaps of impotence (ineffectiveness).

God did not place us here simply to be here. God

did not give us life to misuse or abuse life. On every gravestone there is a date of birth and a date of death and inserted in-between the dates of birth and death is a dash. The dash is representative of life. The dash is representative of all the time we spend or spent alive here on earth. It matters not when we got here and it matters not when we leave here; what matters most is the dash in-between. What matters most is what we have done with our dash. So we understand, we live with our dash every day. So we understand, we give merit or demerit to our dash every day by what we do or neglect to do. Thus, the question becomes: what are we doing with our dash? Thus, the question becomes: are we being fruitful or fruitless with our dash? Think about it. What are you doing with your dash?

Life is meant to impact life. Life is meant to enhance life. The life we live is meant to be the type of life that makes God proud and the type of life that justifies why we are here. Helping people justifies why we are here. Making life better for someone else justifies why we are here. Spreading the Gospel of Jesus Christ justifies why we are here. Winning souls to the Kingdom of God justifies why we are here. Feeding the hungry is a justifier. Serving the homeless is a justifier. Uplifting the disadvantaged is a justifier. Emancipating the shackled is a justifier. When we do what we can with what we have while we are here to supplement the hurts, and the burdens, and the essential needs of those around us in our season of life, then we are making the most of the time we are apportioned by God to be here. In addition, when we do these things, we please God. In addition, when we do these things, we are applauded by God and one day shall hear Him say, "Well done!"

The Word is: "Be careful how you live" (Ephesians 5:15). The Word is: "Make the most of the time" (Ephesians 5:16). The Word is: "Do not be foolish" (Ephesians 5:17). The Word is: "Understand what the will of the Lord is" (Ephesians 5:17). God's will be that we serve Him. God's will be that we obey His commandments. God wills us to live holy. God wills us to walk upright. God wills us to wholeheartedly love Him. God wills us to love each other. He wills us to put Him first. He wills us to go that extra mile. He wills us to platform His cause. God wills us to make time for Him every day—to talk to Him every day—to read His Word every day—to impart His love every day—to represent Him every day. What better way to utilize our God-given time here on earth other than doing God's will. In Romans 12:1-2, the Apostle Paul declares: "I beseech you therefore, brethren, by the mercies of God, that ye present your bodies a living sacrifice, holy, acceptable unto God, which is your reasonable service. And be not conformed to this world: but be ye transformed by the renewing of your mind, that ye may prove what is that good, and acceptable, and perfect, will of God."

Time is of the essence. We do not have time to delay. Time is of the essence. We do not have time to waste. With every tick-tock of the clock, we are running out of time. With every tick-tock of the clock, the windows of opportunity dwindle. We cannot afford to drag our feet. We cannot afford to put off and suspend. We cannot afford to diddle daddle. We cannot afford to play Russian Roulette with time. The sands of time are shifting. The sands of time are slowly fading out of view. You ought not want to get to the end of your life with regrets. You ought not want to get to the end of your life grieving over what could have been done. Make the most of time. Live life to the fullest. Make the most of time. Make use of every moment. Get busy. Do something. Start something. Work your dreams. Stop waiting for something to happen and stop waiting for someone to make things happen for you. Make things happen for yourself. Stop waiting on validation from other people. Learn how to validate yourself. Make the most of time. You may not get a next time. Make the most of time. It may be 'now' or 'never.' Do not procrastinate and do not pause. It is later than we think and tomorrow is not promised to any of us.

Stop saying: "I do not have time," and stop wasting time. Instead, invest time. Invest time in your family. Invest time in your children. Invest time in your marriage. Invest time in yourself. Invest time in Kingdom work. Invest time in Kingdom service. Invest time in Kingdom purpose. Invest time in Kingdom mission. Never forget Who gave us time (God). Never forget why we are here. Never forget why time is given. Never forget that time will tick out. In John 9:4, Jesus says: "I must work the works of Him that sent Me, while it is day: the night cometh, when no man can work." And just like with Jesus, for all of us, nightfall is on the way. Just like with Jesus, for all of us, the sun will set in our lives. Make the most of time. Take advantage of the time. Make the most of time. Manage your time well. If you listen, you can hear the tick-tock of the clock. If you listen, you can hear the sound of time moving on. Listen! It is nonrefundable. Listen! It is nonredeemable.

Make time count. It is all that we have. Make time

count. We only have it for a short while. It is getting late in the evening. Do not let your work go undone. It is getting late in the evening. Do something while you can. Do something with your years. Do something with your months. Do something with your weeks. Do something with your days. Do something relevant. Do something significant. Awake from your sleep. Rise up from your bed. Make the most of time because time is winding up. Time is moving on. Soon, and very soon, our season will be over. Soon, and very soon, our days will be no more. So while we are here, let us make the most of it. So while we are here, let us make an imprint for the Kingdom of God on earth. Let us help somebody. Let us do God's will. Let us broadcast the message and ministry of Jesus Christ. Let us live the type of life that will substantiate the time we are here. Tick-tock, tick-tock. Tick-tock, tick-tock!

"But seek first the Kingdom of God and His righteousness,
and all these things shall be added to you."
Jesus of Nazareth

Chapter Eleven

PUT GOD FIRST

In everything you do, put God first, and He will direct
you and crown your efforts with success.
Proverbs 3:6 TLB

Most people are familiar with the passage of Proverbs 3:6 as it is rendered in the King James Version of Scripture: "In all thy ways acknowledge Him, and He shall direct thy paths." For clarity, we have selected the wording of 'The Living Bible' in order to extract from it the three words of the topic of this chapter: "Put God First." This is the point the wisdom writer drives home in any interpretation or translation of Proverbs 3:6. For understanding, 'The Living Bible' is not a translation of Scripture, but a paraphrase of Scripture.

A "paraphrase" is "an expression of something using different words to achieve greater simplicity." In other words, the purpose of a paraphrase is to say as precisely as possible what the writer means without being vague or unclear. What a paraphrase does in its choice of words is to use more specificity to give us, the reader, an uncomplicated knowledge of what is being said and why. Therefore, instead of saying, "In all thy ways acknowledge Him, and He shall direct thy paths," the paraphrase version of Proverbs 3:6 reads: "In everything you do, put God first, and He will direct you and crown your efforts with success." This statement, as communicated in The Living Bible, is simple and straightforward. This statement, as communicated in The Living Bible, is candid and gets right to the heart of the matter—God first. God first is the blueprint for divine collaboration, supervision, guidance, and for divinely influenced success and accomplishment.

God first is the emphasis of the First Commandment of the Ten Commandments. It reads: "Have no other gods before Me" (Exodus 20:3). God first is the emphasis of the Greatest Commandment. It reads: "Love the LORD thy God with all of your heart, soul, mind, and strength" (Matthew 22:37; Mark 12:30). God first is the emphasis of what I call the Pursuit Commandment. It reads: "But seek ye first the Kingdom of Heaven" (Matthew 6:33). God first is the emphasis of God's Will, and of His Word, and of His Way. Putting God first is doing what God wants us to do 'above' and 'beyond' our own desires. It is submitting to God's ordinances. It is yielding to God's sovereignty. It is surrendering to God's purpose. It is living by God's standards.

In life, there are many things that vie or compete for our attention, allegiance, devotion, and time. Putting God first is placing God before all else and before all others. It is placing God before our spouse. It is placing God before our child. It is placing God before our job. It is placing God before our self. It is placing Him before our mother. It is placing Him before our father. It is placing Him before our sister. It is placing Him before our brother. It is making God the priority in one's life, and it is realizing that God has no equal and shares His glory with no one. Putting God first is giving God preeminence in our lives and lordship over our lives. What is "preeminent" surpasses all others. Who is "lord" is the one who is in charge.

If God is LORD, then God is in charge. If God is in charge, then we seek His direction and obey His command. If we seek His direction and obey His command, then what God instructs us to do, we do. Where God instructs us to go, we go. What God instructs us to say, we say. How God instructs us to live, we live. Putting God first is putting everything that is in our control in God's control. It is giving God control of every personal resource, ability, ambition, and conviction. Putting God first is trusting God with all things and having faith in God for all things. It is giving God our very best and committing to God our total lives.

As the psalmist says: "Order my steps in Thy Word: and let not any iniquity have dominion over me" (Psalm 119:133), putting God first is allowing God to order our daily steps. Putting God first is sanctioning God to do with us what He pleases. It is saying to God, like Jesus said: "Nevertheless, not my will, but Thine be done" (Luke 22:42). It is saying to God, like the Prophet Isaiah said: "Here am I; send me" (Isaiah 6:8). When we put God first, we give God more than lip service. What is lip service? Lip service is a declaration of support, obedience, or loyalty that is merely expressed in words, but not backed up by deeds. To state it another way; it is "faith without works" (James 2:26).

When we put God first, we honor God through action. When we put God first, we do things that validate our relationship with God. We feed the hungry. We clothe the naked. We help the hurting. We involve ourselves in ministry. Ministry is not necessarily what is done inside of the church house on Sundays, but ministry is availing oneself in service to God through service to others, in the Lord's name and to the Lord's glory, between Sundays. Ministry is meeting the needs of people with love and humility. Ministry is continuing the works of Jesus Christ with compassion without bias or discrimination.

Putting God first is giving God first place in our heart, home, relationship, and with our time. Putting God first is talking to God first, seeking His counsel, and searching His Word in search of His Will. It is saying to God, "yes LORD." Christians should live a God first life. Christians must live a God first life. For the Christian, a God first life is mandatory. For the Christian, a God first life is required living. For the Christian, a God first life is a commission and it is advantageous. Putting God first is the secret to a happy and blessed life (Psalm 1). It is the formula for obtaining miracles and for the acquisition of Kingdom favor.

Amazing things happen when God is put first. Supernatural things happen when God is put first. Proverbs 3:6 says: "In everything you do, put God first, and He will direct you and crown your efforts with success" (TLB). When we put God first, we gain God's presence, power, protection, and provision. When we say to God, "Thy Kingdom come; Thy will be done" (Matthew 6:10), and when we "seek those things which are above" (Colossians 3:1), God withholds nothing from us, as God is pleased with us. Note Proverbs 16:7.

Putting God first is the right thing to do and God

first is the right place for God to be. The LORD's name is "Jealous" (Exodus 34:14). God demands allegiance, fidelity, monogamy, homage, and untainted acknowledgement. God cannot be compared to anyone else and God cannot be replaced with anyone else. God first means: God only. God first means: only God. Only God do we worship. Only God do we serve. Only God do we cling to. Only God do we pray to. Only God do we bow before. Only God do we obey. Only God do we defer to. Only God do we trust. Absolute trust is exclusive for God. Psalm 146:3 declares: "Put not thy trust in man."

Putting God first means we trust God, hope in God, wholeheartedly believe God, and totally depend on God. Interpretation: we look to God for help. Interpretation: we seek God for advice. Interpretation: we call on God for direction. Interpretation: we invite God into our lives. We invite God into our problems. We invite God into our worries. We invite God into our circumstances. We invite God into our decisions. We do not move without God. We do not choose without God. We do not begin something without God. We do not complete anything without God. Interpretation: we wait on God. Here is a promise for waiting: "They that wait upon the LORD shall renew their strength; they shall mount up with wings as eagles; they shall run, and not be weary; and they shall walk, and not faint" (Isaiah 40:31).

Why are we dealing with this? Because it pays to put God first. Why are we dealing with this? Because it is strategic to put God first. When God is first: "No weapon that is formed against thee shall prosper" (Isaiah 54:17). "If God is for us, who can be against us" (Romans 8:31 NIV)? When you put God first, you have God. When you have God, you have the resources and angelic forces of God's Kingdom. My advice: do not do anything without God. My advice: do not get married without God. My advice: do not sign a contract without God. My advice: do not say 'yes' to anyone without God. My advice: do not make a destiny decision without God. Consult God. Meditate on His Word. Consider His Will. "In everything you do, put God first" (Proverbs 3:6 TLB).

Put God first with your paycheck. Put God first with your gifts and talents. Put God first with your focus. Put God first with your time. Do not give God your leftovers. Do not give God your spare change. Do not give God your convenience. Give God what God deserves. God deserves the best, the pick of the litter, the crème de la crème, and our optimum ability. Put God first. Give Him your youth. Put God first. Give Him your health. Put God first. Give Him your wealth. Put God first. Give Him your all. God first is God's rightful place. God first is God's required place. God first is God's only place. No other place will do.

If you want to make life count, then wherever you go in life, put God first. Whatever you do in life, put God first. God first puts you first. God first gives you leverage with God. It gives you God's heart and it gives you God's hand. Making God number one in your life is beneficial to your life. Put nothing or no one before Him. Number two with God is never sufficient. God will only acknowledge and accept being first. In English: "Number one!" In Spanish: "Numero Uno!" In French: "Numéro Un!" In Chinese: Zuì hǎo de!" In any language or region, it is still the same: God first! In order to maximize our time on earth, we must put God first and keep God first. Do it! You will not regret it. Do it! God will bless your life.

"Carve your name on hearts, not tombstones. A legacy is etched
into the minds of others and the stories they share about you."
Shannon L. Alder

Chapter Twelve

LEAVE A LEGACY

A good person leaves an inheritance for their children's children,
but a sinner's wealth is stored up for the righteous.
Proverbs 13:22 NIV

In Chapter One we discussed, "Making Life Count," and we mentioned the importance of leaving a legacy. Legacy is what we leave behind when we die and die we will. In Chapter One we stated that we can leave a legacy of beneficial knowledge, deeds, values, and investments. Why end this book on this topic? Leaving a legacy is important and leaving a legacy is divinely encouraged. What we do for ourselves while we are here is well and good. However, what we do for ourselves is gone when we are gone. What outlast our human existence are the things we do or leave for others. This is what prolongs our life beyond the grave. This is "legacy."

All human life will eventually expire, pass away, kick the bucket, bite the dust. But before we do, or before we cease to exist, we should ensure an endowment of some kind for the next generation, especially an endowment for our children, and for our children's children. This is "legacy." Legacy is inheritance, custom, inscription—it is what lives on after we die. Legacy is what continues after we die. Legacy is what endures after we die. Legacy is what survives after we die. Legacy is what remains after we die. It is what remains after the funeral. It is what remains after the burial. It is what remains after the repast. It is what remains after the will has been unsealed and its contents revealed to our loved ones. Legacy is the impact we make on Planet Earth. It is more than what we say. It is what we do. It is how we live. It is who we are.

Most of the time legacy is viewed in terms of money, and if not money, then property. However, money and property are not the only treasures we can bequest upon death. In fact, there are many intangible things that are far more valuable than money or property. The priceless intangibles include: faith, character, integrity, information, memories, life lessons, life stories, and lineage. Lineage is a legacy 'commodity' that too many of our children are not privy to. Too many children are clueless when it comes to ancestry. Many have no knowledge of their father, and some, not even their mother. Many are left with no record of grandparents, or great-grandparents, and some without a legitimate name of their own. By legitimate name I mean—a name that connects them to their rightful ancestors and the name that should be inherited to them as their birthright.

We all have names, but many of our children do not possess the name of their paternal bloodline. The last name of their father is not their last name. Many of them bear the name of their mother's descent. More so than money or property, we ought to leave our children a legitimate name. Why should our sons and our daughters go through life without the ability to correctly trace their descendance simply because the name they bear is not the rightful name they should have. Giving our children and leaving our children our name is "legacy."

Besides leaving our children our name, *legacy* is also the transference of worth. As parents, and as grandparents, we should make sure that our children and our grandchildren know their worth. I am not talking about in terms of dollars and cents, but I am talking about in terms of personal appraisal. Too many of our children and our grandchildren have low opinions of themselves. Too many of them sell themselves short. In other words, they do not give themselves enough credit and they tend to diminish their own capabilities. Far too many of them view themselves as less than other people. This is where "legacy" comes in.

While we are here, as parents, and as grandparents, we should do all that we can to instill within the minds and hearts of our children and grandchildren positive and persuasive assertions about themselves. We should tell them how beautiful they are. We should tell them how intellectual they are. We should tell them how capable they are. We should tell them how significant they are. We should affirm their potential, ability, essence, and value. Like in the book and movie entitled, "The Help," we should say to them, from a very young age: "You is kind. You is smart. You is important" (Kathryn Stockett). This we should say until they believe and affirm such for themselves. I realize that some may criticize the vernacular: "You is kind, you is smart, and you is important." But the point I am making is that we should indoctrinate our children and grandchildren with a vocabulary of expressions that encourages them to be the best that they can be and emboldens them not to allow anyone or any circumstance to make them feel inferior, second-rate, low-class, or stupid. No parent or grandparent should degrade their children or grandchildren. No parent or grandparent should allow anyone else to do so either. As parents and grandparents, we should propel our children and grandchildren to reach for the stars. This is "legacy."

Proverbs 13:22 declares: "A good person leaves an inheritance" (NIV). What is an inheritance? An inheritance are life seeds that are sown which yield harvest beyond our years. It is a tree planted. It is a book written. It is a business established. It is a garden cultivated. It is a wound healed. It is a child taught. It is a grandchild inspired. It is a soul revived and saved. It is faith transmitted. It is love reallocated. It is the Gospel passed down to the next generation. It is the story of Calvary retold. We ought not to exist for ourselves, we should leave a legacy. We should do something worth remembering, write something worth reading, teach something worth learning, and make the world a better place because we lived. We should be a mentor, an inventor, an architect, a benefactor.

Life is about helping to improve the lives of others. Life is about helping others to appreciate life, and to embrace life, and to live! This is "legacy." Legacy is giving an encouraging word, doing an uplifting deed, being an inspiring example, and living an unforgettable existence. It is living life in such a way that people remember us when we leave, miss us when we leave, admire us when we leave, and celebrate us when we leave. Life is short. We need to maximize our time on earth by leaving a legacy. By leaving a fingerprint, blueprint, benchmark, and residue. By leaving some money, property, wisdom, and something useful on the field of life. We ought not live to become legends but live to leave legacies. We should leave gifts from our life, and from our labors, and from our service, and from our reputation. If nothing else, we should leave a good name, example, report, and reputation. We should leave a life that keeps on living and an image worthy of duplication. We should make life count.

Have you thought about it? How will you be remembered? Will you be remembered? What will you leave behind? Will you leave anything behind? I say: "leave a legacy!" Leave something beneficial, constructive, respectable, and gratifying. Do not leave something detrimental, immoral, counterfeit, and unacceptable. When your life has ended and when your story is told, do not let your story be one of fabrication, disappointment, appalling, and deplorable. Do not let it be a wicked story. Do not let it be a criminal story. Do not let it be a despicable story. Do not let it be a disgusting story. Every life tells a story, but make sure that your story is a story worth repeating. Leave a legacy.

Carve your name into the history books. Carve your name into the hall of the decent. Carve your name onto the wall of the righteous. Carve your name within the pages of the "Book of Life." The Book of Life is God's Book. The Book of Life is the Lamb's Book. The Lamb is Jesus, who gave His life for our sins. Jesus left us a legacy that keeps on producing life. If your name is in the Lamb's Book of Life, you will live with God forever and have a place reserved in Heaven. If your name is in the Lamb's Book of Life, you have been redeemed by the blood of Jesus and your salvation has been sealed. How can you be sure that your name is in this Book? Leave a legacy. Leave a legacy of repentance. Leave a legacy of humility. Leave a legacy of service. Leave a legacy of a life that is well lived. If in your life you acknowledge Jesus and make Him Lord of your life and if you defer to Him and allow His Light to shine through your life, your legacy is documented in the Book of Life. And oh, what a legacy!

It pays to believe in Jesus. It pays to live right. It pays to live holy. It pays to trust in God. Leave a legacy of righteous deeds. God keeps reliable records and He knows who belongs to Him. It is God who inserts the names and once we are inserted, we are secure. So, as I wrap up this chapter and this book, I ask you this question: what type of legacy do you want to leave? Your children's future is in your hands and the future of your grandchildren are too. Leave a legacy. The only things we take with us are the things we leave behind. Leave something behind. It is encouraged in Scripture. It is the right thing to do. It is in God's will. Think about who comes next. We cannot and we will not live forever, but we can leave something that lingers on after we die. Let it be something that makes an impact, and something that God will find delight in, and something that will give God glory, and something that will survive the fire test of judgment. Leave a real legacy. Leave a pure legacy. Leave a moral legacy. If you want to hear the Lord say one day, "Well done," then strive in life to do the will of God.

As a people who believe in God here is the message: in life, focus on pleasing God. As a people whose lives are dedicated to God we should make life count, and the best way to make life count is to realize that there is no eternal value in the things of this world. So true is this: Only what we do for Christ will last. Leave a legacy. Make life count! Leave a legacy. Maximize your time on Planet Earth! Socrates said, "Our lives are but specks of dust falling through the fingers of time. Like sands of the hourglass, so are the days of our lives." As time rolls on, the sands are shifting. Do not let the sands of your life shift without doing something worthwhile. MAKE LIFE COUNT!

EPILOGUE

As human beings, we have a brief interval of time here on earth. The Bible reminds us that life is but a vapor that soon vanishes away (James 4:14). This means that our lives are temporary. In other words, we are a mist that is here for a moment and then gone, and with this realization we should neither squander our years of life nor take them for granted. I have endeavored in this book to stress the importance of every second, minute, day, week, month, and year that God blesses us with life. I have endeavored in this book to persuade and encourage every reader to use every second, minute, day, week, month, and year to MAKE LIFE COUNT.

Our earthly existence is sandwiched between two dates: our birth and our death, and in between these dates on the headstones of our grave is a dash. The dash is representative of our time span of life. The dash is representative of what we accomplish or fail to accomplish with our life. Life matters, and how we utilize life is important. What is also important is our understanding of why we are here. In Chapter 2, I addressed this subject by pointing us back to God. God is the reason we are here and our lives are given meaning as we live our lives in God's purpose. As I stated in Chapter 2: "every life has purpose." We simply need to discover our purpose and fulfill it.

Many people struggle with discovering their life's purpose. Some people never discover their life's purpose.

This is a tragedy. It is a tragedy to go through life without ever discerning why you are here. It is a tragedy to near the end of one's life without some sense of feeling that your life meant something. I have endeavored in this book to assist you in navigating your life journey into purpose. I have endeavored in this book to help you in your discovery of purpose and in your implementation of purpose. If you did not get the point—discovering purpose begins at God. No life exists without God and no life's purpose is fulfilled without the inclusion of God.

Writing this book has been a labor of love with a desire to inspire someone to make the most of every opportunity to enhance life by extracting from life all things that are detrimental to life. This was our focus in Chapters 4, 5, 7, 8, and 9. In order to maximize life, we need to make wise choices and decisions, associate with the right people, travel down the right roads, not dwell on the past, and stop procrastinating. Most importantly, we must not be wasteful with the valuable God-endowed resources of time, talent, and treasure. This is made easier when we put God first. This is made easier when we apply the instructions of God's Word to our lives. The Bible says, "Trust in the LORD with all your heart, and lean not on your own understanding; in all your ways acknowledge Him, and He [God] shall direct your paths" (Proverbs 3:5-6 NKJV).

Do not be guilty of taking life for granted. Do not be guilty of misappropriating life by not making the most of life in the way that God intends for us to live. How does God intend for us to live? God wants us to love Him wholeheartedly. This is the first and greatest commandment: "And you shall love the LORD your God with all your heart, with all your soul, with all your mind, and with all your strength" (Mark 12:30 NKJV). God also wants us to love others. This is the second greatest commandment: "You shall love your neighbor as yourself" (Mark 12:31 NKJV). The Bible says, "There is no other commandment greater than these" (Mark 12:31 NKJV). Life is made richer when we recognize the place of God in our lives and that place is first. Life is also made richer when we do what we can to improve the lives of others.

Let not your life be wasted. Let not your life be a blur in the memory of those who knew you and even to those who did not. Make your life count! Maximize your time on earth! Make an impact! Live life with no limits and leave a lasting legacy behind. Remember: with every tick-tock of the clock life is passing. Remember: "you only live once, but if you do it right, once is enough" (Mae West). Never forget: we are living to live again. Never forget: what we do in this life determines our placement for the afterlife (Heaven or Hell). My advice: live a quality life. My advice: live a meaningful life. My advice: let God be pleased with your life. My advice: live your life so well that God will compliment your life at the end of your life with these words: "Well done!" Better yet, with these words: "Well done, my good and faithful servant!" MAKE LIFE COUNT!

The moment we have now will never
come again. Make the most of it.

MAKE LIFE COUNT

Larry A. Brookins

For more publications by Larry A. Brookins visit:

www.labrookins.org

Printed in the United States
By Bookmasters